Living by the Sea

Christine Desmoulins

LIVING BY THE SEA

25 international examples

Birkhäuser
Basel · Boston · Berlin

I would like to thank all the people, near and far, who provided invaluable help in the development of this book, in particular:

Frédéric Lenne, director of the Architecture, Engineering, and Urbanism department at Groupe Moniteur, for authorizing access to that collection; Valérie Thouard, head of the architecture division, and Raphaëlle Roux, editor, for their commitment to me during the long development of this book; Hadrien Bartherotte, president of Cabanes Bartherotte & Frères, Marion Cloarec, manager of development at CNDB, and Roland Dallemagne, consultant, former representative of CIMbéton and former managing editor of *Construction moderne*, for their scientific advice given during the preparation of the technical appendices; Mathilde Billaud, Sandra Barclay, and Jean-Pierre Crousse for their help in gathering data.
And finally, thanks to all the clients and architects who showed me their built work and to all those at their firms who shared their time with me.

Graphic Design
Isabel Gautray
Joëlle Leblond

Cover Design
Alexandra Zöller

Translation from French
Elizabeth Kugler

Lithography
FAP

Printing
Chirat

Library of Congress Control Number: 2008922533

Bibliographic information published by Die Deutsche Bibliothek
Die Deutsche Bibliothek lists this publication in the DeutscheNationalbibliografie; detailed bibliographic data is available on the internet at http://dnb.ddb.de.

The French edition of this book was published under the title "25 maisons en bord de mer" by Editions du Moniteur, 17, rue d'Uzès, 75108 Paris Cedex 02, France

Printed on acid-free paper produced from chlorine-free pulp. TCF ∞

Printed in France
ISBN 978-3-7643-8695-5

www.birkhauser.ch
9 8 7 6 5 4 3 2 1

Contents

The Popularity of the Seaside

It all begins with a legendary house...

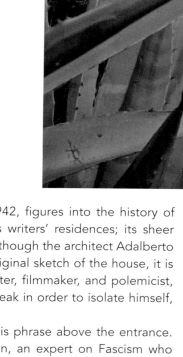

Le Mépris (Contempt) by Jean-Luc Godard, 1963, a confrontation between classic cinema and modern cinema, with Homer's *Odyssey* and the role of producers as background.

The Casa Malaparte in Capri, built between 1938 and 1942, figures into the history of twentieth-century architecture and the register of famous writers' residences; its sheer poetic force makes it the most legendary seaside house. Although the architect Adalberto Libera (1903-63), a leading Italian rationalist, signed the original sketch of the house, it is above all the work of Curzio Malaparte (1898-1957), a writer, filmmaker, and polemicist, who chose to situate the house on an inhospitable rocky peak in order to isolate himself, write, and find refuge.

Casa come me (A house like me) – Malaparte inscribed this phrase above the entrance. The house does indeed reflect the personality of this man, an expert on Fascism who was long imprisoned on the Lipari Islands for denouncing Mussolini's direction and Hitler's rise to power. He also founded a journal to which Picasso, Joyce, and the Dadaists contributed.

Camped out on a steep and reputedly unbuildable site at Punta Massullo, the house establishes osmosis – an effortless flow – between the building and a natural setting of exceptional beauty. Inspiration came from many sources. Besides the rationalist reference, Casa Malaparte borrows from classical architecture without breaking with the simplicity of the terraced houses of the Amalfi Coast. The monumental exterior staircase leads to the roof terrace, an unenclosed sun patio sheltered by a curved screen, where Malaparte used to ride his bicycle. The trapezoidal staircase, which directly echoes that of the Church of the Annunciation in Lipari, also built on a rocky slope, evokes the architecture of an open-air theater as well.

Like the very spare interiors, where large bay windows frame the sea and the reefs as if they were paintings, the sun-bathed staircase and terrace fascinated the movie director Jean-Luc Godard, who picked this site to shoot *Le Mépris* (Contempt), of 1963, starring Brigitte Bardot, Michel Piccoli, Fritz Lang, and Jack Palance.

Curzio Malaparte wanted a modern house in "the most beautiful landscape in the world." The villa, which was abandoned for a long time after his death, has finally been restored and is accessible once again.

To Live and Build by the Sea

Shacks, cabins, houses, huts, villas, or other types of residences – everybody is fond of the house that shelters them. In Western societies, the single-family house, which fulfills our desire for ownership and for freedom, is preferred over collective housing, for it gives substance to one of life's ideals. For the architect, the subject is complex but captivating, and houses designed by the greatest names punctuate the history of architecture.

Eclecticism under the sun

From fishermen's cottages built with the materials at hand to merchants' villas in the large maritime ports to the white prisms on the Greek islands and the mansions of seaside towns that were fashionable in the nineteenth and twentieth centuries – the ground is rich in terms of original styles and typologies. This is true in many places: the Anglo-Norman and

Catherine Proux, restoration of Sarah Bernhardt's fort at Belle-Ile-en-Mer, Brittany, France, 1894/2006
In 1894, to satisfy her need for a vacation home, the famous tragedienne Sarah Bernhardt acquired a fort at Belle-Ile-en-Mer, near the lighthouse on the Ile des Poulains. This military post became her summer residence, and for her friends she built two houses (the Villa des Cinq Parties du Monde and the Villa Lysiane), as well as a studio; the architecture was rustic, but functional and radical. Except for the studio, which no longer exists, this group of buildings joins the natural sites of Brittany protected by the Conservatoire du littoral (Coastal Protection Agency), and the fort is listed in the Supplementary Inventory of Historic Monuments. Recently, the three buildings were renovated by the architect Catherine Proux, who set out to preserve the character of the site.

Arne Jacobsen, the Rüthwen-Jürgensen House in Skodsborg, Denmark, 1953-56
Arne Jacobsen earned a place in the history of architecture by linking the ideas of the Modern movement and the techniques of traditional Danish architecture.
Four kilometers north of Copenhagen, this large house, built for a coffee importer, consists of three wings, oriented so as to optimize the panoramic views while at the same time delineating a sheltered courtyard.
The main wing has a steel structure; the other two are of rendered brick. A teak curtain wall incorporating the ventilation grilles sets the stage as the house opens onto the landscape.

Mediterranean coasts, the Basque Country, the Anfa hill in Casablanca, as well as in Florida, California, and the bay of Rio. To the greatest pleasure of movie directors and romantic spirits, the Baroque and Art Deco mingle with Modernism, and the most cutting-edge compositions can be found beside works that borrow from colonial typologies.
With Robert Mallet-Stevens, Eileen Gray, and Jean Badovici, southeastern France saw the birth of seaside modernity in the 1920s. The United States stood out as one of the melting pots for this in the 1950s. Today, all eyes turn willingly toward Australia, Japan, South America, and the countries of northern Europe.
Whereas, in a permanent dwelling, many owners favor heritage value, comfort, and security, on the seaside, the drama of the landscapes, the contact with the elements, and the vacation mind-set leave more room for pleasure. The warmth of the walls and the terraces in the light, the framing of the grandiose views, proximity and distance, the cool feeling of a layer of stone, the stirring shadows of a pergola – architecture and sensuality come together, but when the beauty of the setting becomes menacing, one must also confront the wind, the sea spray, and the stormy skies.

Shoei Yoh, a house on the sea in Japan, 2000
Dreaming of a glass house perched over the sea, the architect Shoei Yoh built his house on a 150-meter-high cliff, with a splendid view of the Tsushima Islands and Ikonishima. The villa is secured to the ground by two thick concrete walls, and the cantilevered living room overlooks the sea. On the eastern façade, translucent glass panels maintain privacy. The ocean façade consists of glass panels without casements held in place by steel rods and silicone joints.

Gert Wingårdh,
Villa Nilson in Varberg, Sweden, 1992
A bird's-eye view of the villa and its site, and the long glazed façade protected from the sun by a pergola.

Jean-Paul Viguier, restoration of the Villa Eden in Tamaris, La Seyne-sur-Mer, France, 2006
Following administrative difficulties encountered while building a modern house of his own design in Sospel (in southeastern France), Jean-Paul Viguier decided instead to restore a crumbling Italo-Asian-style house on the hills that overlook the sea, facing the harbor in Toulon. It is part of a group of eighty houses, most of them designed by Paul Page in the late nineteenth century in the Tarmaris neighborhood, founded by Marius Michel (called Michel Pacha); only a few of these houses survive today. In restoring this house, Jean-Paul Viguier was as faithful as possible to the original style and form – a very challenging task, for several pieces were missing. The sloping garden was redesigned to create terraces supported by walls made of stone from Borme.

To live and to contemplate

If the house goes back to the idea of shelter, what drives an individual to choose an uneven, isolated site rather than a better-protected space?
The need to commune with nature or to own an unusual site, the desire to isolate oneself, to spend some silent moments in contact with the elements or to jealously appropriate a landscape as if it were a work of art – these are some explanations. To look out on the sea or plunge into it, to inhabit the landscape, to forget the everyday life in summertime or to spend one's life facing the ocean – there are many reasons to build a house by the sea, where romanticism, modernity, the log cabin myth, and nomadic and temporary settlements all mingle... Everywhere, seaside houses cling to the cliffs, leaving a mark on the headland; others crouch on their sites; still others dip their feet in the water. The result is houses that are very diverse in terms of architectural vocabulary, shape, structure, materials, and scale. Nevertheless, the architects must vie for the cleverest way to anchor the house on uneven terrain that changes in appearance with the rhythm of the tides, to raise the house to a panoramic viewpoint, to capture or tone down the bright light, to open the space to the outdoors while at the same time protecting the envelope from wind and bad weather, even if it means nestling the house in relief or making some façades opaque.

Kengo Kuma, the Water/Glass House in Atami, Japan, 1995
This guest house built on a layer of water and perched over the ocean accompanies a large house atop a cliff on the Pacific side of Japan. The guest house features three rooms linked by laminated glass bridges. Accessible by a glass staircase, the floor of the uppermost, third level is covered with a 15-centimeter-deep layer of water, upon which three glass boxes are positioned. To create visual continuity between the floor of the living room and the ocean, this level consists of two sheets of safety glass laminated together. Illuminated at night, the house seems to be floating on the water. The glass tables and chairs do not disrupt the view. In 1997 this design won the AIA DuPont Benedictus Award.

In this book, we single out contemporary houses that stand out for their uniqueness and for the complexity of the site. Exuberant, minimalist, or unusual – they all, through their formal and technical inventiveness, highlight the clients' architectural wishes. They use the most innovative materials and technologies, as well as traditional know-how and the resources of vernacular architecture.

Spaces for living or contemplation, architectural promenades, frames that capture the views – seaside vacation houses offer great opportunities for experiment. Often complemented by detached guest houses, gardens, terraces, and swimming pools that extend naturally toward the water or toward nature, they give rise to interesting compositions. In terms of function, the rooms tend toward versatility, a flexibility that responds to the changing needs of the residents. While making daily life run smoothly, the built-ins refine the space. And as urban nomads sometimes work better when they are on vacation, the houses also include libraries or offices, and sometimes the bedrooms turn into studios. The Bastion House in Coliumo, Chile (see page 78), partially escapes its domestic status; another house in Peru plays aquarium (see page 132). Elsewhere, several generations of a family share the common spaces (see page 44). In Japan, folded shapes and origami mix (see pages 64 and 98). In Dungeness, Great Britain, a trailer serves as the guest bedrooms (see page 112), and in Antiparos, a house mimics a crater (see page 146).

Sean Godsell, house at Saint Andrew's Beach, Australia, 2006

To wrap simple volumes in a lattice skin that regulates light and heat is a recurring principle in the designs of Sean Godsell. This particular design is a weekend house for a family of four on the Mornington Peninsula. A block propped up on steel pilotis houses the living room, kitchen, three bedrooms, and their bathrooms. Parking and storage are under the house. The oxidized steel outer skin hinges open to form brise-soleil shutters.

Donati Dubor Architects, house in Corsica, France, 2007

This house occupies a large parcel in an old development, where the clients wanted to build a contemporary house. To that end, the architects recycled the slab of an existing structure and built retaining walls with drystone cladding. Because of thermal constraints, only one area forges a connection between interior and exterior: the kitchen/living area, approximately 100 square meters, with an immense window measuring 7.4 by 2.2 meters. This room thus finds its echo in the terrace, set under a bamboo pergola that disappears in winter.

While adapting their work to the topography and appropriating an existing staircase, the architects knew how to vary the viewpoints.

Brian MacKay Lyons, double house on La Have Estuary, Canada, 1998

By introducing into an estuary two buildings in tension, Brian MacKay Lyons has punctuated a landscape whose meaning he respects. Consisting of a living area and a guest house aligned on a north-south axis, this ensemble overlooks La Have estuary, in Canada. At night, the two structures, linked by concrete walls, bring to mind the lanterns in the two lighthouses facing, on one side, the estuary, and on the other, the ocean. The marshy land that separates the two units provides a garden, open to the local fauna.

To build in a sensible setting: technical and regulatory constraints

At the edge of the sea, the choice of where to situate the building on a given site, the question of materials, and that of exposure with regard to the prevailing winds are crucial factors. Sustainable development and pragmatism prevail with regard to construction, conservation, and upkeep; as much as possible, local materials and techniques that are well adapted to the particularities of the sites and climates are preferred, as shown in the examples presented in the second part of this book. For these sensitive sites, where sometimes only a strip of land can accommodate construction, it is imperative to choose the best possible orientation for wind protection, to capture the heat in winter and, by contrast, promote natural ventilation in summer. An examination of the topography and a rigorous geological analysis will determine the nature of the foundations. In some cases, antiseismic foundations or retaining walls are required. When building a house, it is necessary to anticipate the maintenance costs: because the regular repainting of the exterior, for example, can prove expensive, permanent and easily maintained materials are recommended. In fact, it is advisable to protect the structure from corrosion caused by sand and salt air. In this area, the quality of the workmanship and the details of execution, as defined by the architect and carried out by the contractors, are the best guarantee of a good result; the same is true for the choice of adequate materials, whether concrete, steel, wood, polymer, glass, or copper.

Philippe Vion, house in Assérac, France, 2004

At the tip of Pen Bé Peninsula, the house looks over the sea on three sides. The architect played with the rules of urbanism, picking up the architectural grammar of Brittany, such as the slate ridge roof, while accentuating the austere features of the traditional forms: the harshness of blue-gray cladding, the absence of visible profiles, such as rainwater downpipes or other details.

The height restrictions dictated the overall shape and the location of the terrace above the garage. From this terrace, which is protected from the prevailing winds, the ocean is visible on two sides.

It is impossible to build everywhere, which is why it is important to protect parts of the coast. In terms of ecology, the coastlines – the land-sea interface and the meeting point for fresh and salt water – constitute a rich palette of natural settings and landscapes, which are very sensitive to the changes inflicted by human activities. Many nations take steps to try to find a just equilibrium between the conservation of these areas and their economic development (see the appendix, page 158). In France, to accompany the Coastal Act of January 3, 1986, the Conservatoire du littoral (Coastal Protection Agency), a public organization created in 1975, acquires delicate and threatened land, which it restores before entrusting the management to local authorities under its control. Thus in June 2006, the agency ensured the protection of 100,000 hectares on 400 sites, that is, 880 kilometers of waterfront.

Everywhere in the world, conflicting private interests are unfortunately often opposed to conservation measures. In Asia, it is known that preserving the mangroves helps reduce the effects of tsunamis, and that the tsunami on December 26, 2004 hit hardest the area where real-estate development had destroyed these moist areas. Similarly, on August 29, 2005, Hurricane Katrina affected the American coasts and the Gulf of Mexico especially in areas where the petroleum industry had encroached on the marshes. In Europe, the concreting of the coasts through industry, tourism, and pressure to build has also had devastating effects on ecology, in particular by aggravating soil erosion.

Philippe Robert (Reichen & Robert), a group of houses in Kérénoc, France, 2007
A high point between sea and land, a sharp point with granite outcrops, beautiful trees, reliefs, a sloping prairie, and the hollow of an old quarry protected from the wind... The houses, gathered in groups of four or six, fit in with the rocks and among the trees; their siting takes into account both insolation and views. The project promotes the use of natural materials (wood and concrete frame, wood façades, organic roofs) and integrates a bioclimatic approach (cross ventilation, full shutters, thermal inertia of the roof for comfort in summer, large bays exposed to the sun, and fireplaces in the large volumes for comfort in winter).

Gerson Castelo Branco, house on Dos Poldros Island, Spain, 1993
Log cabin art and the legend of Robinson Crusoe set the tone on the Canary island of Dos Poldros, with this ecological wooden vacation house featuring irregular shapes. It overlooks a 1,200-hectare site planted with carnauba palms and dense vegetation that goes down to the sea. The carnaubas supplied the building material, both the boards and the thatch roof.

The struggle against the elements and soil erosion

Before building a house a few meters from the sea, it is necessary to know the possible impact of the phenomenon of soil erosion. Due to the disturbance of the hydrosedimentary system on the coasts, the erosion of beaches occurs throughout the world, and many countries have set out to find a solution. As any intervention in one area can have a negative effect several kilometers away, in-depth studies are needed. Fortunately, not all coastal land is affected. For example, a granite site covered by a thin layer of dirt, such as the site of the House on a Snowy Promontory in Canada (see page 60), is not subject to erosion.

At the tip of Cap Ferret, a paradise that evokes the legend of Robinson Crusoe, an epic undertaking by Benoît Bartherotte illustrates the issue of conservation of sensitive land affected by marine erosion. On this narrow peninsula that is exposed to the currents, fishermen's houses made of pinewood are a tradition. In the past, they used to be disassembled and moved back a bit when the sea encroached on the land. Facing Cap Ferret, the seaside resort of Arcachon was built in the nineteenth century, with the arrival of the railroad. Since that time, the prevailing current moving toward the tip of the headland has caused it to retreat by more than one kilometer in fifty years.

The owner of part of this headland, Benoît Bartherotte, and his family built three very simple houses on the site, made of wood and inspired by the local structures and by buildings with verandas, a typology imported to the region by contractors returning from the colonies. In 1985 he launched a fight against erosion by building a 150-meter-long seawall, which he has continued to strengthen ever since. He is gradually recovering the land and, on the reconquered ground, he plants pine trees and insular vegetation to hold the ground in place.

Richard Texier, a fishing hut in Aytrée Bay, near La Rochelle, France, 2003

Starting in the nineteenth century, in the Charente-Maritime region of France, fishing with a square net mounted on a frame gave rise to the construction of huts set on platforms several meters above the shore, to which they were linked by a floating dock. Apart from the anchoring of the piles in the earth, these curious structures on stilts, whose heritage value is established, have not been excavated.
Moreover, after a big storm in December 1999, many had to be reconstructed. Richard Texier entrusted the construction work on his fishing hut to Serge Roussel, of the Escabel firm, and his colleagues. The daily challenge was to take advantage of the low tide to sink into the earth (at a depth of 1.5 meters) three portal frames, then link them via 13.5 meters of walkways and, at high tide, to climb the walkway in order to do the surface treatments. One hundred fifty cubic meters of ekki, a siliceous ironwood that becomes petrified in an ocean environment and whose density reaches 1,200 kilograms per cubic meter, were used. "This cabin, which is 12 cubic meters, has nothing in common with the setting that inspired it. It is a simple studio between earth and sky, a modest refuge that I rebuilt as an art installation in the middle of the ocean, a geomantic site for my work." His one-hundred-meter-long pontoon is one of the longest, having a depth of 3 meters at high tide. Richard Texier, an international painter, sculptor, and nomad, takes refuge in this poetic place to read, draw, and paint.

If the concept of using a seawall to detour the current, trap sand, and re-create natural soil is relatively simple, in practice it is a Herculean task that is also extremely expensive; Bartherotte has already invested nearly 5 million euros. At the rate of 25 tons per meter, there is almost continuous activity, with trucks discharging thousands of tons of concrete and recycled rubble into the channel in order to refill the underwater talus. As in a game of Mikado, beams and railroad ties strengthen the ensemble while ensuring better cohesion of the rockfill, yet without eliminating the risk of collapse. An official report issued by the Port of Bordeaux and by Sogreah (the former Central Hydraulic Laboratory of France) recognized the utility of such a step, which led the State representative to declare, "The private interest of Benoît Bartherotte is much the same as the general interest," for this work also protects from submersion a whole section of the peninsula and its housing developments. Although Cap Ferret is now subject to financial pressure that is altering the beauty of a long-protected site, Benoît Bartherotte took a stand against the housing-development mentality and enhanced the value of a long-neglected landscape.
Beyond conservation of natural areas in the strict sense of the term, what should we make of the planning regulations that are supposed to protect the beauty of the landscape? To enact legislation without a minimum of knowledge and sensitivity is questionable. Everywhere in the world, we find that makeshift structures can contribute to the charm of coastal landscapes, whereas regulated development often changes it despite the restrictive specifications. In many coastal areas in France, a paradoxical situation has arisen. Sprawl in the countryside attributable to low-quality developments continues with the pink plaster "Play Mobile"-type houses. To obtain a permit to build a contemporary house, however, often proves so difficult that clients become discouraged. And yet a contemporary house situated away from the towns is likely to add even more value to the most beautiful landscape.

Benoît Bartherotte, house at the tip of Cap Ferret, France, 1998
At left, the large house borrows colonial typologies. From the floor to the walls of the bathrooms, all the surfaces are in untreated pine. Below, Benoît Bartherotte's seawall at work.

The Beautiful Americans

Modern houses by the sea and the superb cars of their owners are among the icons of postwar America. California and Florida provided conducive ground for seaside modernity, and the upturn in the economy strongly contributed to the development of a new architecture and a new way of life in contact with the landscape. Starting in 1945, John Entenza, editor in chief of *Arts and Architecture*, gave the movement decisive momentum by launching a program of 36 prototype homes, the Case Study Houses, to propose a new aesthetic as an alternative to the traditional residence. Designed by major architects such as Richard Neutra, Charles and Ray Eames, Pierre Koenig, Craig Ellwood, and Raphael Soriano, these experimental houses, which were supposed to be mass-producible, relied on the use of building systems and prefabricated materials from modular components. Most of these projects were not actually built, but some were constructed in the San Francisco Bay Area, in Hollywood, and in Beverly Hills, for instance.

One of Paul Rudolph's concerns was to wed structure and form. A former disciple of Walter Gropius at Harvard, he started his career in Florida, where, between the 1940s and the 1960s, he built a whole series of houses equally representative of American modernity.

Although the reference to Mies van der Rohe and the spirit of the International Style prevailed in the Case Study Houses, John Lautner, a former student of Frank Lloyd Wright, became famous in the 1970s and 1980s for astonishing houses that blended organic influences and technological breakthroughs. Form and structure merged, and the landscape – natural or artificial – became a full-fledged component of the architecture. Presenting to the ocean emphatic concrete curves and glass walls, these free-form houses are worthy of the ideals of the architect and the dreams of an elite clientele.

Paul Rudolph, Burnette House in Sarasota, Florida, 1949-50
Inspired by the reinforced-concrete houses of the European avant-garde, the Burnette House, with a structure linking concrete and steel, is characterized by the freedom of its plan and by its spatial abstraction. The walls and the roof are plane surfaces of the same thickness.

Paul Rudolph, Hook House in Siesta Key, Florida, 1952
Facing the sea and surrounded by tropical vegetation, the Hook House was built for Mary Rockwell Hook. For the first time in a design on a domestic scale, Rudolph used a plywood vault. Partitions, sliding bays, and movable Venetian blinds make the house a space with variable geometry.

Paul Rudolph, Deering House in Casey Key, Florida, 1956-58
Open to the sea, the living space derives its rhythm from nine columns whose thickness contrasts with the transparency of the windows. The structure of the house had to be especially strong to withstand the destructive force of the seasonal storms.

John Lautner, Beyer House in Malibu, California, 1975-83
With its immense faceted bay windows and a roof with many undulations, the Beyer House faces the ocean directly. The plan found its inspiration in the movement of the waves; the living spaces are strung together fluidly, and the undulations in the plane find echoes in the staircases, the circulation patterns, the mezzanines, and the built-in furniture. The framing of views and the architect's incorporation of rock draw the landscape into the interior of the house. The project took eight years to complete because the state and the California Coastal Commission wanted to take back the land. For budgetary reasons, the roof, originally intended to be concrete, is in fact a wood frame with plaster ceilings.

John Lautner, Arango House in Acapulco, Mexico, 1973
One of Lautner's masterpieces, the Arango House overlooks a hill facing the Acapulco bay.

On the Mediterranean Shores

A crossroads for many cultures, the Mediterranean is a mirror across which a great diversity of styles pass – from Rome to Damascus to the Greek islands, Barcelona, and Tunis. From the intersection of all these influences came an eclectic architecture, where Baroque and Art Deco are sometimes tinged with Orientalism. The prosperity of the basin made many merchants rich, and some of them built veritable palaces, which are the charm of the coastal towns. At the same time, the resort appeal encouraged great diversity in domestic typologies. Buildings of substance and depth where one moves from dazzling light to dimness, Mediterranean structures use the light and color of the setting.

In the early twentieth century, the pioneers of Modern architecture found inspiration in the geometry of flat-roofed houses, the cleanness of whitewashed walls, and the purity of the original forms. The villa designed by Mallet-Stevens on the upper slopes of Hyères for the Count and Viscountess de Noailles is proof of it, as are the beautiful, exciting undertakings of Le Corbusier, Eileen Gray, and Jean Badovici at Roquebrune-Cap-Martin. Since then, the shores of the Mediterranean continue to inspire architects. The house built by Silvia Gmür and Livio Vacchini in Greece attests to this, as do the works by Marc Barani, Antoinio Citterio, and Deca Architecture, which are shown in the second part of this book.

Robert Mallet-Stevens,
Villa Noailles in Hyères, France, 1923-33
In 1923 Charles and Marie-Laure de Noailles gave Robert Mallet-Stevens his first big commission: the design of a vacation house on their property Clos Saint-Bernard, on the upper slopes of Hyères. The villa, inhabited as of November 1925, would continue to be enlarged until 1933. Many artists contributed to the décor of this little modern heliotrope palace with its terraces, its covered pool in reinforced concrete with sliding glass partitions, and its cubist garden laid out by Gabriel Guévrékian. Owned by the City of Hyères and since 1987 listed in the Inventory of Historic Monuments, the villa was recently restored by architects Cécile Briolle, Claude Marro, and Jacques Repiquet and today houses a cultural meeting center.

Eileen Gray and Jean Badovici, E 1027 House in Roquebrune-Cap-Martin, France, 1926-29
Eileen Gray wanted to create a "functional architecture in which beauty is useful…, an architecture for the modern man." Captivated by De Stijl and by the work of Le Corbusier, she and her partner, the architect Jean Badovici, built a large functionalist villa resembling a white ocean liner. Decorated with frescoes by Le Corbusier, this house is part of the heritage of the Modern movement. With the Roquebrune-Cap-Martin District competition, it was acquired by the Conservatoire du littoral (Coastal Protection Agency) in June 1999. A restoration campaign from 2007 to 2009 will ensure its definitive protection and make it possible to open the building to the public.

Le Corbusier, hut in Roquebrune-Cap-Martin, France, 1952
For Le Corbusier, poetry was "a phenomenon of rigorous exactitude," as evidenced by his hut, a reinterpretation of its counterpart in Marseilles and of the cabins in the Canadian forests. The hut is a finished, freestanding space measuring 3.66 by 3.66 by 2.26 meters. Conforming to the rules of the Modulor, it is fitted out with built-in furniture that makes clever use of the space and is decorated with frescoes. Le Corbusier drowned on August 27, 1965, off Roquebrune.

Silvia Gmür and Livio Vacchini, house in Greece, 1994-98
A long rectangular plane joins two similar but reversed volumes, a succession of voids and solids, and white walls that slope to capture the reflections of the light on the water – this sums up the seaside house built in Greece by Silvia Gmür and Livio Vacchini. The simplicity of volumes and the play with inversion and slope transform our perception of each space, but also of the countryside and of privacy. The garden entrance, terraces, living room, kitchen, porch, courtyard planted with palm trees, bedrooms, and bathrooms are connected, with varying orientations and openings.

Han Tümertekin, SM House in Turkey, 2004-6
In a context a bit like that of the building shown in the second part of this book, the architect Han Tümertekin built another vacation house on the outskirts of an Aegean village. Opening onto an imposing landscape and onto the sea, the house abuts a road with a massive wall of stone. Taken up again on the roof, the stone envelops the house to frame the views. In this project, the architect explores the theme of permeability – both real and visual – of a living unit where open, semi-open, and enclosed spaces follow one another all along the north-south axis. All the rooms are on the same level. To make this long structure sturdy, prefabricated steel components form the frame, which is itself supported by curtain walls.

Massimiliano and Doriana Fuksas, conversion of agricultural land into vacation houses on the island of Pantelleria, Italy, starting in 2003
To look not at the countryside, but at the sea – this was the intention of the architects Massimiliano and Doriana Fuksas, who transformed an old olive grove into a site for vacation homes. In Pantelleria, they gradually converted a dozen *dammusi*, or rural houses. Built over time starting in the fifteenth century, the *dammusi* are characterized by simple volumes, a vaulted structure, and thick drystone walls. Perfectly adapted to the climate and to their agricultural function, they were originally pierced with small openings. Intent on respecting the structural logic, the spirit of the place, and the beauty of the rustic materials, the architects enlarged some of these openings and created others opposite them to allow air to circulate naturally, eliminating the need for any artificial ventilation. They also proposed terraces oriented toward the sea. Through this discreet shift of the vernacular architecture, they carried out a subtle, contemporary intervention in an immutable context.

Durbach Block Architects, house in Australia, 2004
When the sea and a desire for modernity meet, the result is sometimes a contained exuberance, and this house serves as a superb illustration. White volumes, retaining walls, low walls, and drystone stairs cascade down the hillside and over the rocks to the ocean. The swimming pool stabilizes the composition, sited as it is on a horizontal terrace, also mineral, in which the shape of the pool introduces new variations. With the waves directly ahead, a permanent contrast is established between the curves, undulations, and sharp angles, on the one hand, and, on the other, the more radical large square glass side walls. The spare white interiors and the terraces open wide to the sea, as if to draw it indoors – a plastic, dynamic view of the relationship to the ocean.

Smiljan Radic, house in Taraconte, Chile, 2003
A magnificent dialogue between architecture and nature, the house and its contemplative pool mix mineral substance with transparency, traditional structural solutions with the most up-to-date technologies. The architect distributed the volumes and the functions according to the curves of the levels in order to procure varied sensations. Traversing the site is a staircase starting at the road, 40 meters above sea level. Lower down, a plateau parallel to the coast receives the access platform to the house and a ramp descending toward the terrace, where the pool was installed for a panoramic viewpoint. Lower still, touching the shore, is a block reserved for the children. Terraces and volumes in suspension, staircases and sheltered courtyards are strung together, one after the next. The contrast between equilibrium and disequilibrium feeds the relationship to the site. The function of these volumes and their terracing makes it possible to occupy them more or less intensively depending on the season.

Corona y Perez Amaral Arquitectos (Antonio Corona Bosch, Arsenio Pérez Amaral), house in Tenerife, Canary Islands, Spain, 2006
A glass and concrete monolith, the house is set on a wooden platform at the corner of a 300-meter-high cliff, revealing a superb view: a black-sand beach, Mount Teide, and the entire north coast of Tenerife Island. The prism of the bedrooms was added next to a double-height volume housing the living room, a studio, and the kitchen. These two wings are in an L shape around an infinity pool placed in the corner of the platform so that the water in the pool appears to merge with the high tide from the sea. The mirrorlike surface of the water and the wood on the ground frame the views, which can be seen from all the rooms of the house.

1 The House on the Promontory

House with a Panoramic View in the South of France

Atelier Marc Barani

"This house works on two scales," says Marc Barani. "It is a powerful, material presence on the scale of the site; at the same time, it effaces itself and becomes transparent and fluid, providing the greatest possible freedom in the living spaces. It is at once a belvedere, intertwined with the view and an anchored, protective place. In this project, it was a matter of finding a new harmony between the spatial experiences, between architecture and landscape – in other words, proposing a very specific way of experiencing the landscape, of living in it, of inhabiting it."
Stretched out on the slope facing the sea and the path of the sun, this vacation house for a well-to-do couple with two children is in the tradition of vacation homes in the South of France. Communal spaces and areas to receive guests (living/dining room, playroom for the children, billiards room, television room) are situated in the untreated concrete boxes secured on the site via a stone plinth. Further to one side, the bedrooms are suspended on the upper floor by a "bridge" building that touches the ground on the upper, more private garden area. Though the architectural layout has the simplicity of a bar superimposed in a U shape, it creates complex interior and exterior spaces that maintain specific relationships with the landscape and the vistas.
As if it were a figurehead for the house, the living room deliberately blurs the boundaries between indoors and outdoors. The floor-to-ceiling windows running around the living room totally disappear into the floor, creating a space that reaches toward the sea via the two horizontal planes of the cantilevered roof and the plinth. "It is an ambiguous place at the interstices between the domesticity of the interiors and the power of the exterior spaces. Depending on whether the place is enclosed by windows or open to the landscape, the overall feeling of the house changes. Open, the house captures nature, lets nature inside. The living spaces change scale, gaining in freedom of use and in fluidity," concludes the architect.
The bedrooms, entirely glazed on the south and on the north, literally let nature pass through; they are intertwined with the light and the landscape.
A system of opaque and translucent filters makes it possible to maintain privacy.
Conforming to antiseismic standards, the house links two types of structure: steel for the cantilevered canopy – which reaches 12.5 meters in span – and the "bridge" building, which is reinforced-concrete for all the volumes anchored to the ground. The use of composite materials for the covering of the canopy made it possible to resolve the thermal and acoustic issues while maintaining the lightness.
Elsewhere, composite panels, stone, and concrete go so far as to be mixed through the handling of details and the layout of components: the stone is grained like the wood, and the size of the composite panels is identical to those of the concrete formwork. Finally, the use of house automation made it possible to manage security and the mobility of the façades, as well as the energy necessary for heating and air conditioning.

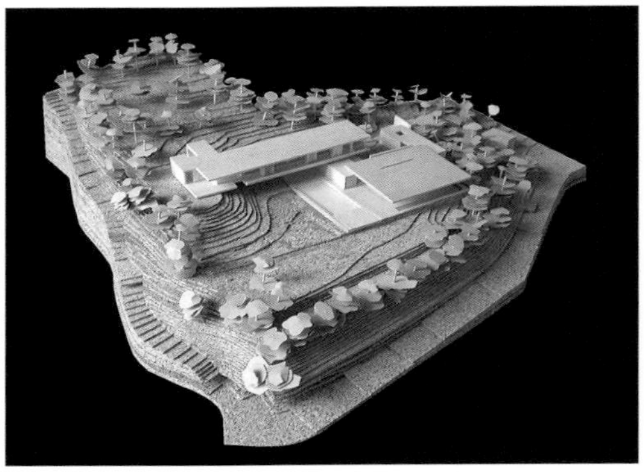

Location: South of France — Program: house, swimming pool, and caretaker's cottage; in the U-shaped building, a living room, billiards room, kitchen, playroom for the children, television room, pantry, patio, and garage; in the "bridge" building, six bedrooms, seven bathrooms, a loggia, and a spa — Owner: private — Architect: Atelier Marc Barani; Marc Barani, architect; Cyril Chênebeau, project manager; Michel Pautrel, project director; Alex Amarrurtu, Julie Assus, Stéphane Fernandez, Éric Jensen, Erwann Lefranc, Ivry Serres, Tetsuo Goto, associate architects; Mireille Bompard, Franck Bosh, Claire Dugard, Philipp Kuehne, Thomas Klemet, Marine Le Goff, Henning Schirmer, Andreia Caetano, Ricardo Latoeiro, assistants; Éric Benqué, designer; Gilles Belley, associate designer; Gilles Clément, landscape architect; François Navarro, assistant landscape architect — Technical consultants: for steel, Arcora; for concrete, A. Pons; for fluids, Enerscop — Surface area: 650 m^2 net living space — Cost of work: not disclosed — Schedule: construction, 2002-04; completion: May 2004 — Building system and materials: concrete and PRS steel structure; untreated concrete and stone façade on an aluminum and epoxy alveolar structure; glazed façade with steel and stainless-steel profiles, wood, exterior ceiling with an alveolar polyester structure, stone floors, interior wood floors and joinery — Contractors: building structure and envelope, steel structure, excavation, waterproofing, VRD, Léon Grosse; heating, ventilation, air conditioning, plumbing, EM; electricity and house automation, CPCP; metal joinery, Chiri; mechanized joinery with vertical retraction, MAS; cladding on the façades and hard floors, SPI International; partitions and linings, Artea; design, Sigebene and Ballestra; wood joinery, Bonelli and MPP; paint, Didier; polyester ceiling, Artec; swimming pool, GP Construct; parquet, Parquet & découverte; kitchen specialist, Boffi.

The roof and terraces stretch toward the sea. The horizon line structures our perception of the building.

A series of PRS 500 steel components form the structural layer of the cantilevered roof. Designed as a series of gutters, this structural layer makes it possible to respond to planning constraints by freeing up the water downpipes.
The underside is clad in honeycombed polyester, and the top of the roof is a honeycombed aluminum composite joined to a thin layer of stone. All of the selected materials are resistant to the coastal atmosphere. In the reinforced-concrete parts, the steel frame was set back further than usual.

The kitchen/dining area.

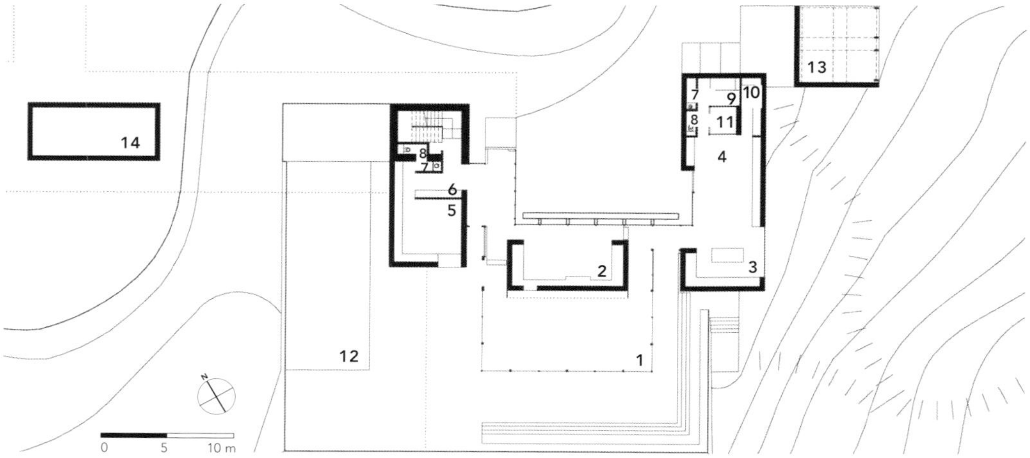

Plan of the U-shaped building
1 living room
2 billiards room
3 kitchen and dining area
4 playroom
5 television room
6 dressing room
7 WC
8 bathroom
9 nanny's room
10 pantry
11 patio
12 swimming pool
13 garage
14 equipment room

In this large house, many specific activities are available to members of the family and their guests. Here, the billiards room.

In the living room, extended by a large cantilever 3.2 meters from the ground, the horizon is at midheight. Nature is captured rather than framed.

White walls, hardwood floors, and wood joinery in the bedroom wing.

The far end of the "bridge" building opens to the landscape through a glazed side wall.

The bathrooms and the spa are arranged so as not to lose visual contact with the sea.

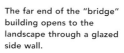

The landscape extends through the "bridge" building, which houses the bedrooms.

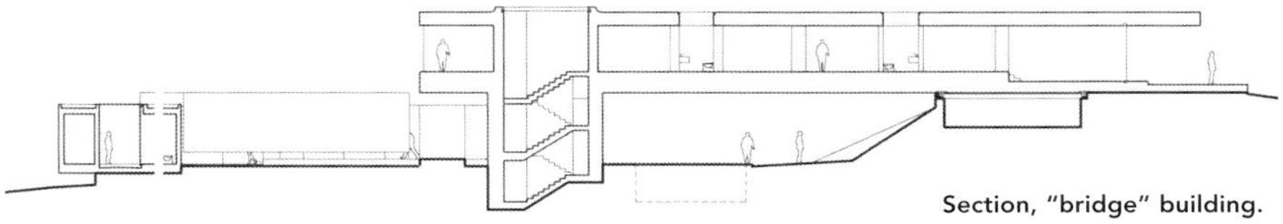

Section, "bridge" building.

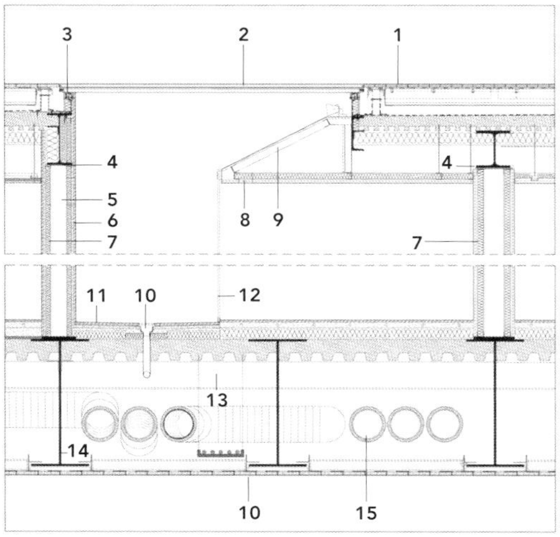

Section showing a detail of the "bridge" building

1 teak roof covering
2 glass roof (210 x 210 cm)
3 metal joinery
4 sound joint
5 metal windbracing
6 stone panels on an aluminum and epoxy alveolar structure
7 two sheets of plasterboard and insulation
8 false plasterboard ceiling
9 metal structure and plasterboard covering
10 shower drain
11 stone facing
12 shower screen
13 IPE 200
14 PRS 900
15 air-conditioning shafts

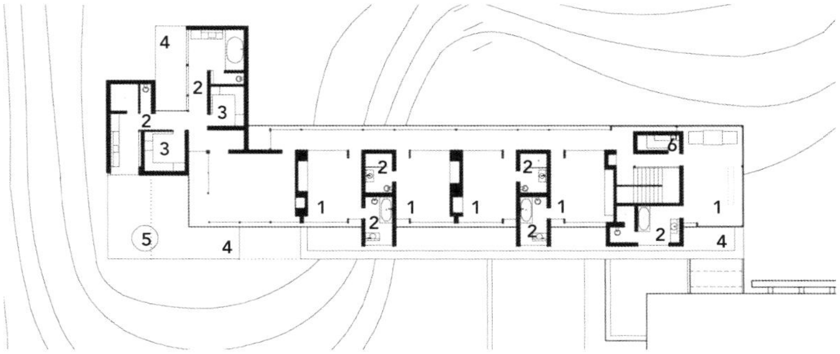

Plan of the "bridge" building

1 bedroom
2 bathroom
3 dressing room
4 loggia
5 spa
6 office

Telescope House, Cape Schanck, Australia

Denton Corker Marshall

On the coast of Australia south of Melbourne, this vacation house and its studio extension resemble a long horizontal tube suspended between the bush and the sea, creating a constructed landscape that echoes the natural setting. According to the designers, the building brings to mind an "unusual object rotated along its axis and ready to touch down" at the top of a steep site bordered by a golf course. Drawing on the color palette of the surroundings, the building has tonalities ranging from charcoal to green to brown.
The main house, which is raised, features ocean views. It consists of two superimposed boxes: the upper floor is cantilevered over the tree canopy. Tilted to adapt to the slope of the site, this very simple gray rectangular form is unique. From its wall panels, set at a slant, and the equally slanting cut of the lower-level windows, the house draws a dynamic that underscores the emergence on the diagonal of the chimney. Set in a niche in the upper box, the entrance is marked by a concrete staircase set in a glazed entryway.
The mixed structure brings together a galvanized steel framework, concrete slabs, and suspended ceiling. The exterior is clad with cement sheets with the joints showing. In the face of very harsh climatic conditions in the region where the winters are cold and very windy, the surface area of the windows was kept to a minimum; their simple glazing was enough to ensure good insulation.
On the interior, in contrast with the white walls and concrete floors, the cruciform beams in galvanized steel reveal the structure. They punctuate a continuous linear space where the boxes clad in maple wood with built-ins delineate the various functions (living, meals, sleep). In the enormous living room that dominates the house, a band of windows unveils spectacular views.
Opposite the windows is a steel panel supporting the chimney foyer, and a hidden sliding door separates the master bedroom and its bathroom. The laundry room and two other bedrooms share the lower level. The two gables, which are entirely glazed, reveal the full extent of the bush country while also establishing visual continuity between the house and the studio, which was conceived as an extension of the main building, from which it is separated by a courtyard.
Built five years after the main house, the studio faces the rear entrance. One can look right through the studio, which is glazed on both ends, where the entrances are located. The ground of the courtyard is an extension of the interior, and a bench, also in concrete, creates a new oblique angle. The central space houses, in an aluminum cube, the kitchenette, the closets, and the bathroom. If necessary, the studio could easily be transformed into a guestroom.

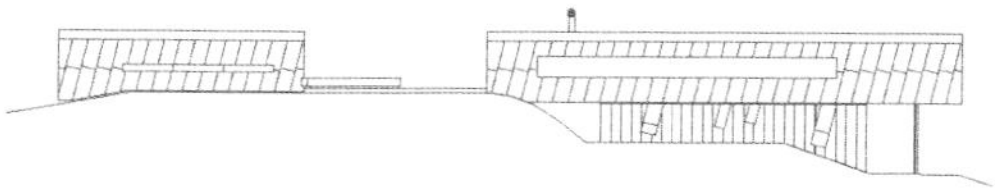

Location: Cape Schanck, Victoria, Australia — Program: two-story house with three bedrooms, two bathrooms, a kitchen, dining room, living room, a laundry room, with a studio pavilion — Owner: Garry Emery — Architect: Denton Corker Marshall — Technical consultants, for structure: Burns Hamilton + Partners — Surface area: house, 197 m² net living space; studio, 60 m² net living space — Cost of work: 728,000 euros — Schedule: house, 1999; studio, 2004 — Building system and materials: galvanized steel structural frame, concrete floors, cement sheet walls, butyl roof, interior surface treatments in plaster — General contractor: for the house, Crest Building Cie; for the studio, Perrin Constructions Pty Ltd.

Balancing on the slope of a hill and rising from the ground with a cantilevered structure on pilotis, the house aims to get above the trees to frame the sea. The main entrance is on the lower side of the volume, behind a glazed screen.

The rear entrance to the studio, where the envelope creates a border and a sheltered threshold.

Between the house and the studio, the courtyard with its bench set at an oblique angle.

Ground-floor and upper-floor plans
1 bedroom
2 bathroom
3 kitchen
4 dining room
5 living room
6 laundry room
7 studio/office
8 small living room in the studio
9 entrance
10 terrace

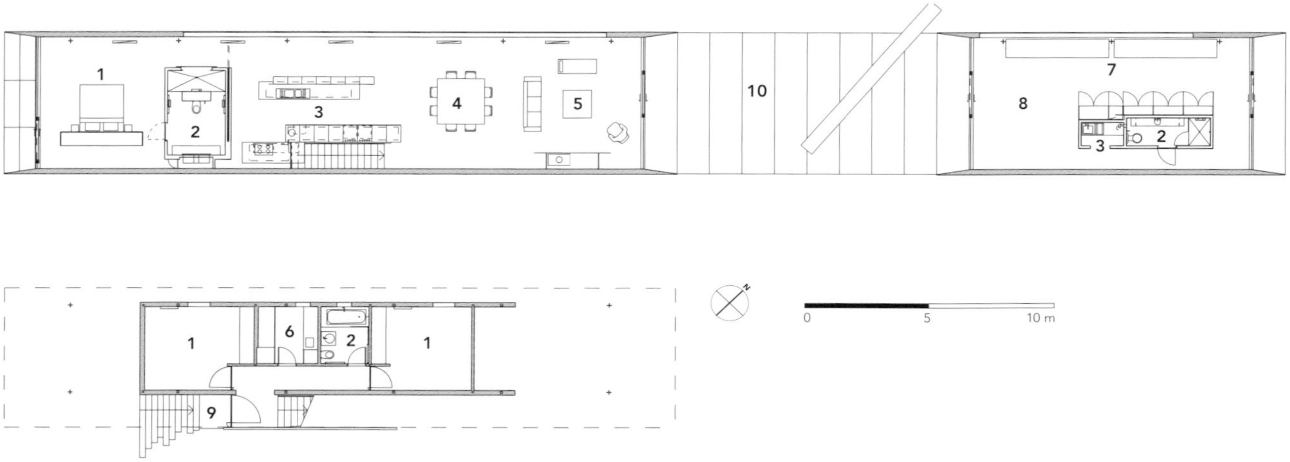

The small living room in the studio.

Cross section showing the galvanized steel frame and the concrete slab.

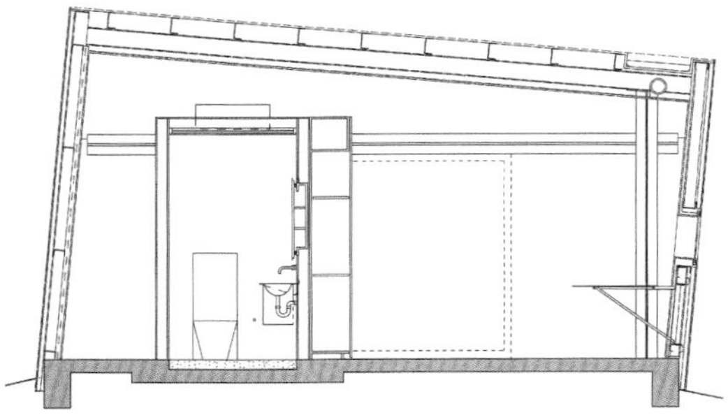

The rear of the house, seen from the studio.

When one is seated in the living or dining room, the horizon is at eye level. A steel panel incorporates the fireplace foyer.

Upside-Down House in Los Vilos, Chile

Cecilia Puga

While this curious structure stacks up volumes whose simplicity brings to mind the little houses in Monopoly, it is the result of serious reflection on the flexibility of a building over time. According to the architect, its form and structure were inspired by the abandoned stations that line the railroads in northern Chile: after the materials had been looted, all that remained was the structure, a container without contents whose concrete walls were punctured with rectangular openings.

In the residence designed by Cecilia Puga, the shape, the unity of materials, and the total absence of surface treatments create the plastic identity of a basic structure where silhouette, color, and texture are inseparable.

The project was also the result of a particular program. To bring together in a single dwelling several generations of a large family, the architect deliberately separated the various functions so that each person could independently adapt the space to his or her liking. Thus at the design phase, the program was divided into three distinct wings, the first for the kitchen/dining area, complete with a loggia; the second for the living room, a bedroom, and a bathroom; and the third for bedrooms, each having its own bathroom.

The research led to a design for three monolithic containers in reinforced concrete, each 5 meters wide. The very spare volumes are punctuated by a series of bays wedged on a 1.2-meter grid. This modular system permits the most varied arrangements to link the volumes together without any hierarchy. In the present case, the layout of the three modules was not really determined in advance; it was the result of a dialogue that took place in the design phase between the architect and her client, even as the foundations, involving the construction of a platform as close to the sea as possible, were being laid. In order to diversify the sea views, the client finally opted for a two-story house, instead of aligning the three pavilions on one level, horizontally. This decision establishes varied relationships between the landscape and the interior spaces while also freeing up the ground, thus preserving the continuity between the site and the sea. Apart from the spiral staircase in prefabricated concrete, which leads to the kitchen/dining area in the upper volume, the three pavilions are linked only on the exterior. The sloping roofs in reinforced concrete, serving as structural beams, emerge in the form of gables. They support the cantilevers, freeing the longitudinal façades from any structural role.

From the kitchen to the terrace, the interiors, free of beams and abutment piers, flow fluidly into the terrace. The openings cut in the untreated concrete underscore the geometry.

Location: Los Vilos, Bahia Azul, Chile — Program: house for a large family with several generations, comprising a first unit for the kitchen/dining area and a loggia, a second for the living room, bedroom, and bathroom, and the third for three bedrooms and their bathrooms — Owner: Barbara Larrain — Architect: Cecilia Puga — Surface area: site, 5,000 m²; building, 200 m² — Cost of work: 110,000 euros — Schedule: 2001-03 — Building system and materials: reinforced-concrete structure, concrete floors and tile, aluminum and galvanized steel joinery — General contractor: Constructora R y H Ltd.

This house is the result of assembling three modules of the same shape. Two of them fit into the ground floor, while the third is superposed upside down.

The house, alone on the rocks, facing the sea.

View from the terrace that opens to the dining room, and the entrance to the bedroom unit.

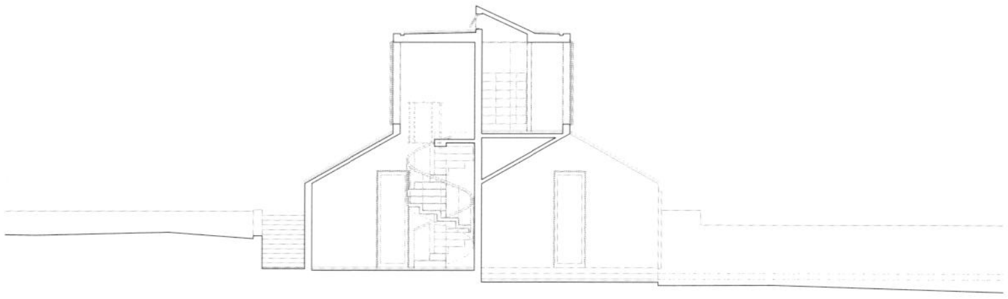

Cross section.

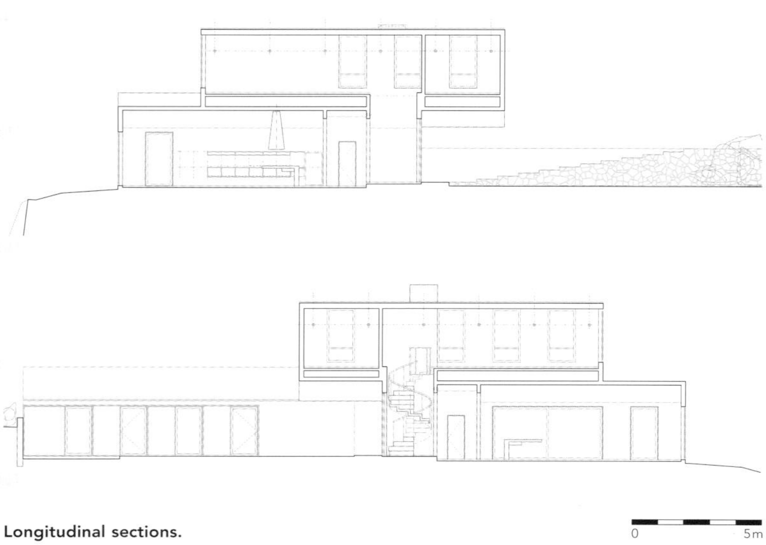

Longitudinal sections.

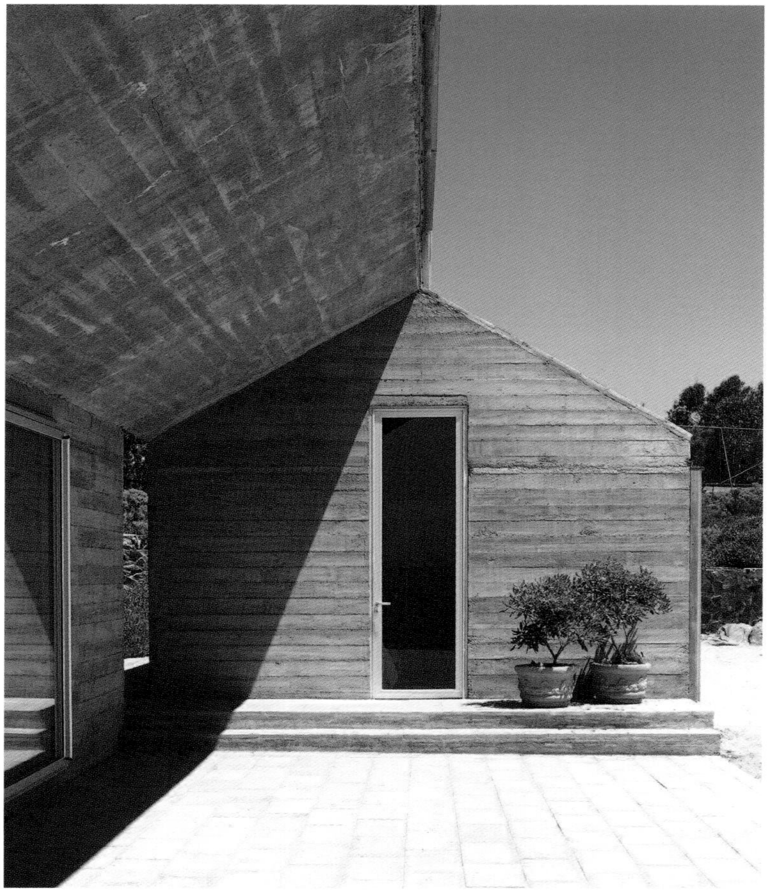

The living room and the corridor, on the upper floor. Antique and contemporary furniture mingle on the untreated concrete floor.

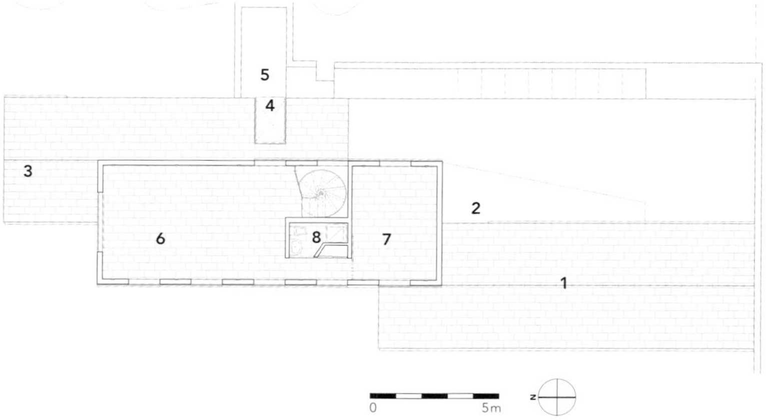

Plan:
Bedroom unit (lower level)
1 bedrooms and bathrooms
2 terrace

Kitchen/Dining unit (lower level)
3 kitchen/dining area
4 entrance
5 loggia

Living-room unit (upper level)
6 living room
7 bedroom
8 bathroom

A large kitchen adapted to the lifestyle of a multigenerational family.

Filter House in Plettenberg Bay, South Africa

Seth Stein Architects

Set a bit away from the Plettenberg Bay beach, on the west cape of South Africa, the parcel is situated in a land of dunes that run down to the sea and are covered with dense vegetation. When the client decided to build this house, it was a relatively isolated site; since that time, urbanization has gained ground on the dunes, but, thanks to its orientation, the house still has very private views of the panorama.
To build in South Africa requires the use of local techniques and materials, such as untreated or polished concrete and wood. Here, the architect mixed concrete with poles of eucalyptus wood, a solid natural material resistant to corrosion in the sea air. Very specifically delineated, the original concrete structure expresses itself powerfully and offers a counterpoint to the irregular texture of the eucalyptus poles, whose color gradually changes to silver gray.
In the 280-square-meter house intended for a family of four, a cantilevered bridge gives all the bedrooms, which are on the second floor, ocean views. Situated in a land where one searches for both shadow and privacy with regard to the exterior, the house is very closed on the street side. The enclosing walls of the ground floor, dominated by the suspended box, are an integral part of the overall composition: they define the parcel and frame the exterior spaces. One of them, slid under the bedroom box, then goes back down to an angle in the swimming pool, creating a porch with a fountain. Opposite, another wall provides the backdrop for a beautiful, fully mature tree.
The architect organized two types of spaces on the totality of the parcel: some rooms are closed and surrounded by solid walls with sliding bays; others form simple outdoor shelters protected from the sun by the cantilevered slab of the bedrooms or set a bit apart from it, in the shade of the eucalyptus poles. These poles are used throughout the site, on the interior as well as the exterior, as facing, as walls, and when attached to a frame by simple copper threads, as wall-screens. A very light, movable palisade that lets in the wind covers the entire length of the bedroom floor, over 23 meters.
Comparable to the cannisse that is indigenous to Provence, eucalyptus poles are used as fencing material in South Africa. Contributing to the architectural aesthetic of the house, they are here promoted to a more noble role. They also constitute a good method of natural ventilation for a dwelling lacking any air-conditioning system.

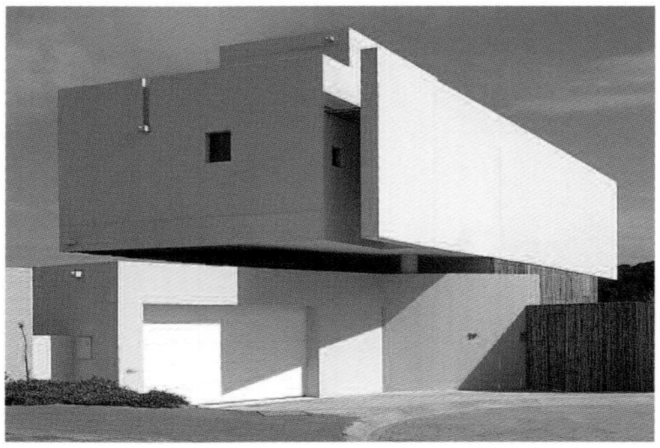

Location: Plettenberg Bay, South Africa — Program: two-story single-family house with swimming pool, terraces, and garage, comprising a living room, kitchen, four bedrooms, and four bathrooms — Owner: private — Architect: Seth Stein Architects — Surface area: 280 m^2 net living space — Cost of work: not disclosed — Schedule: design studies, 2002; construction, 2003; completion, 2004 — Building system and materials: concrete structure; windows, screens, and cantilevers in eucalyptus wood — General contractor: TBC.

In the living-room extension, the outdoor terrace provides shelter with a thick cantilever covered with eucalyptus poles.

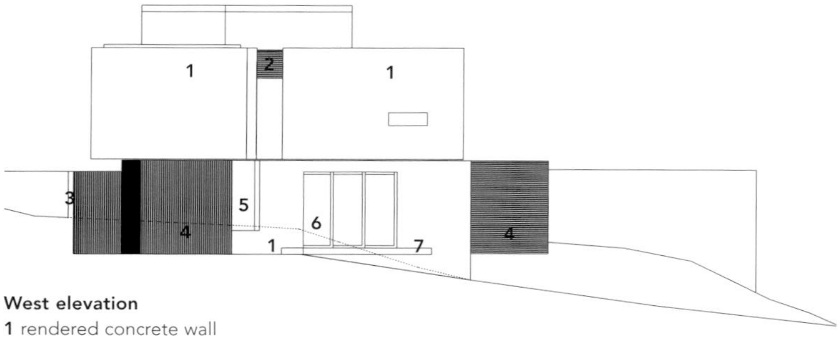

West elevation
1 rendered concrete wall
2 brise-soleil
3 retaining wall
4 eucalyptus screen-partition
5 window without frame
6 sliding French window in aluminum
7 cantilevered concrete slab

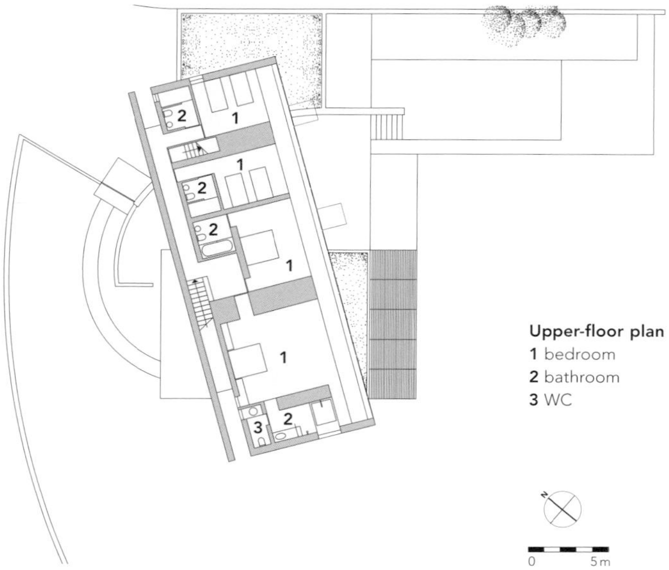

Upper-floor plan
1 bedroom
2 bathroom
3 WC

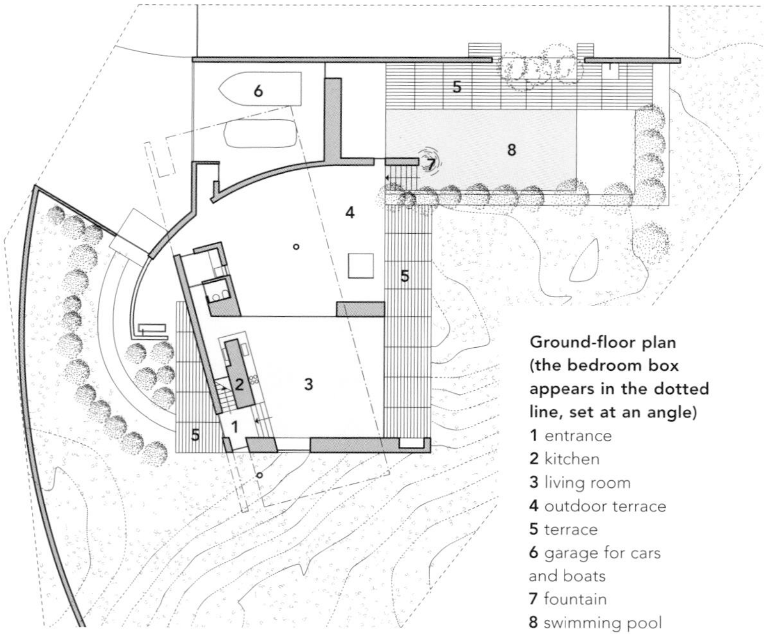

Ground-floor plan (the bedroom box appears in the dotted line, set at an angle)
1 entrance
2 kitchen
3 living room
4 outdoor terrace
5 terrace
6 garage for cars and boats
7 fountain
8 swimming pool

The eucalyptus-pole canopy filters light to provide coolness.

There is a contrast in materials between the white walls and the eucalyptus-pole partition screens, which define the outdoor spaces.

The protruding bedrooms, with the windows open.

Frame House in Canakkale, Turkey

Han Tümertekin

Located a bit away from a small village on the Aegean coast overlooking the sea, the house for brothers Selman and Süha Bilal creates a fitting context for observation of the landscape and immersion in nature. "It involved shaping a space adapted to modern nomads who are very interested in new information technologies and who stay here only occasionally. In choosing this place and observing the environment through the prism of their house, the two 'citizens of the world' thus become village folk; their house finds its correct placement on the hillside, between an olive grove and the sea. They wanted a temporary dwelling, easy to maintain and designed around locally available materials and the know-how of village craftsmen." The contemporary architectural vocabulary of the house takes this into account even if, for Han Tümertekin, this is not really "a local structure." By drawing on both the Modern roots and those of vernacular architecture, the house fits delicately into its setting. In 2004, it earned the architect an award from the Aga Khan Foundation, which gives prizes for buildings and projects involving restoration, urbanism, and planning.

In an area with meandering farming terraces, this building is anchored by two terraces on a triangular parcel accentuating a 7-meter change in level from north to south. The larger terrace, which is rectangular and faces the sea, accommodates the house; the other one, which is triangular, holds the garden in the rear. Although, like the other houses in the village, the building settles into the topography, it also sets itself apart from it by doing away with all fencing, and thus stands out in the landscape like a sculpture on its pedestal. The building derives its character from its formal simplicity and from the contrasting materials that mix industrial components with materials found on-site. The main structure is untreated concrete, poured in place; the filling, in drystone walls installed by hand, is extended for the roof. On the upper level, the steel-frame balcony has wood flooring that continues on the interior. For easy upkeep, the architect used aluminum joinery for the window sashes and shutter frames, with the latter then filled by a woven rattan that provides shade and coolness in summer.

The same contrast exists on the ground floor, where mosaics are mixed with the natural stone. As the budget was relatively small, the interior is spartan; an outdoor staircase links the large ground-floor living room to the two bedrooms upstairs. In order to maintain the spatial purity of these nearly empty rooms that are in contact with nature, a 1.2-meter-wide secondary strip brings together the kitchenette, two bathrooms, the laundry room, closets, and a fireplace. It opens onto the outdoor summer dining room, sheltered under the staircase landing.

Location: Canakkale, Turkey — Program: vacation house comprising a living room, two bedrooms, two bathrooms, a kitchenette, a laundry room, an outdoor dining area, and a garden — Owner: Selman and Süha Bilal — Architect: Mimarlar Tasarim Ltd., Han Tümertekin, architect; Eylem Erdinc, project manager; Ziya Ildiz, Hayriye Zozen, Ahmet Onder, assistants — Surface area: site, 600 m² net living space; building, 150 m² net living space — Cost of work: 100,000 euros — Schedule: development, 1999-2000; construction, 2000-01 — Building system and materials: untreated poured-in-place concrete, stone, steel, joinery in aluminum, rattan, glass, and wood — General contractor: Enver Akan, head mason and carpenter.

In this house with a refined design, the choice of materials serves the architecture. With this house looking out on the sea, the idea of contemplation takes precedence over the idea of a home.

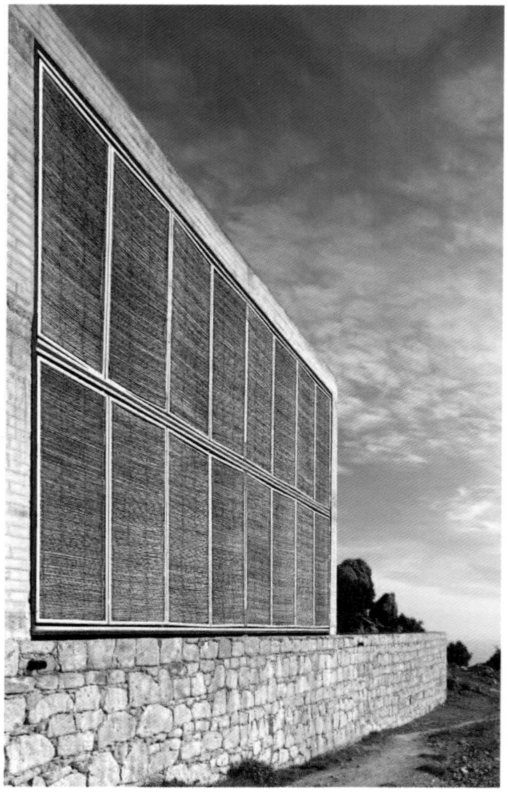

Rudimentary materials suffice for the surface treatments: untreated concrete surrounds the stonework; the aluminum frame for the shutters has rattan trim.

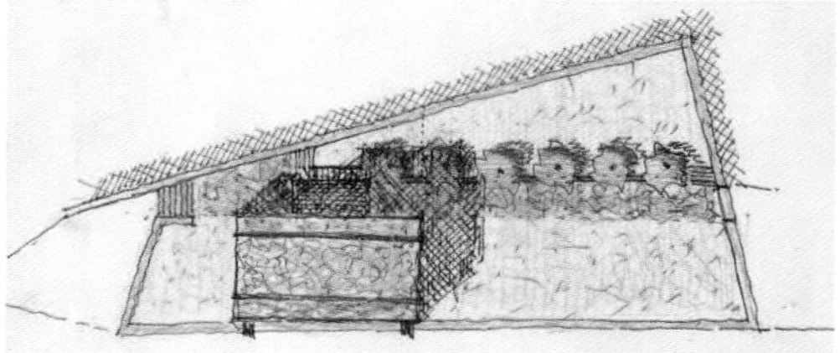

The entrance, summer dining room, and access staircase on the rear façade, near the garden.

Drawing of two terraces which constitute the lot and a landscape study.

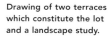

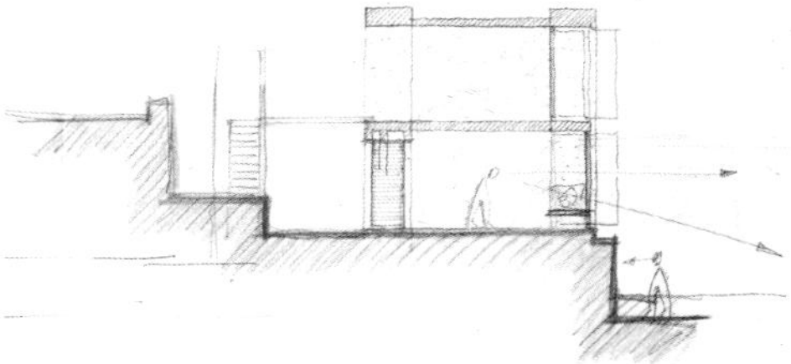

The cross section drawing made it possible to adjust the frames.

One of the challenges was procuring the materials on site, complementing them with manufactured products such as the aluminum joinery for the windows.

A FEW WORDS FROM THE ARCHITECT

"How can a prism create its own landscape? The limits of the site determine those of the interior and exterior spaces of the house, but also those of the walls and levels. To find on-site all the building materials and to complement them with manufactured projects was one of the great challenges of this project, in which the idea of the frame reappeared at every stage of the design. We used all the materials in their natural state and surrounded their contours by other, more refined materials; we thus married stone and untreated concrete, wood and steel, rattan and aluminum. This house, built by Turkish artisans with elements borrowed from vernacular architecture and techniques, is not completely 'local.'"

Construction detail; the manufactured components blend with natural materials and poured-in-place concrete.

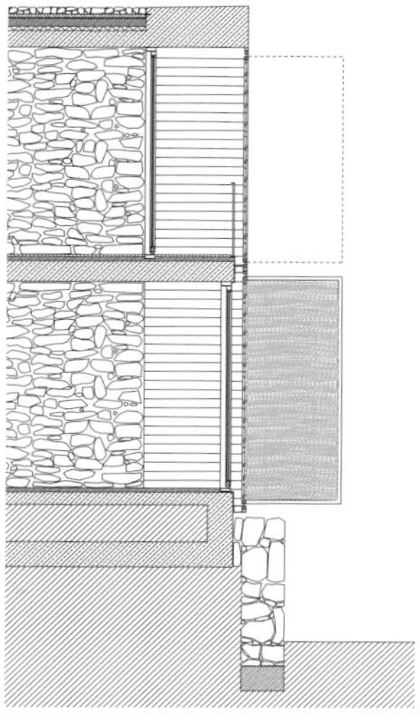

Ground-floor plan
1 living room
2 kitchenette
3 entrance
4 outdoor dining area

0 5m

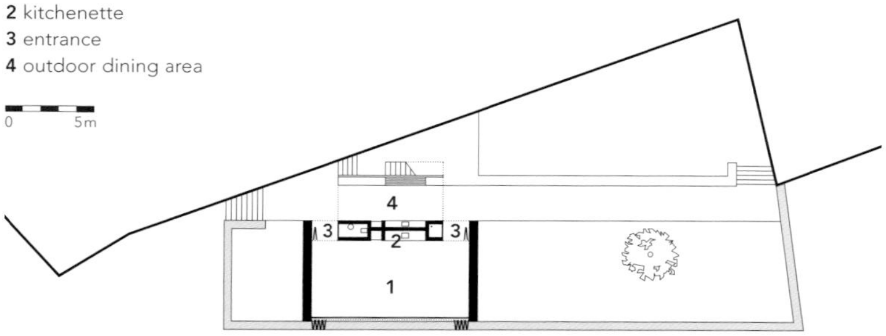

Upper-floor plan
1 balcony
2 bathroom
3 bedroom
4 laundry area
5 storage space
6 balcony over the sea

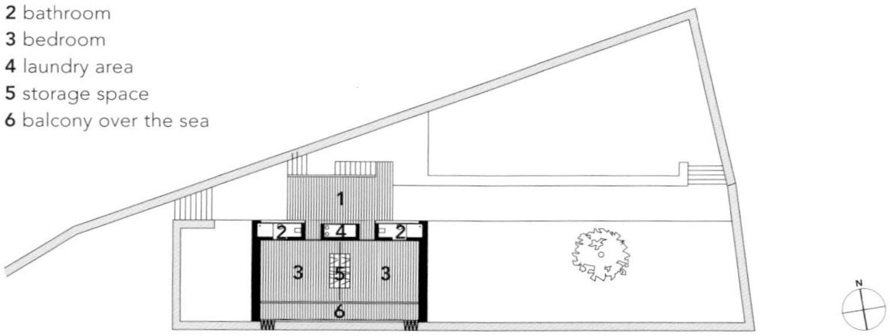

The ground-floor living room. The house becomes a prism to capture nature.

Opposite page:
In summer, the balcony serves as an extension of the two bedrooms; there, light is filtered by the rattan blinds. In winter, the glass wall creates a greenhouse effect.

House on a Snowy Promontory, New Brunswick, Canada

Julie Snow

On the Bay of Fundy, New Brunswick, on the east coast of Canada, the temperature dips to minus 8 degrees in winter, a blanket of snow covers the ground forty-five days a year, and the thermal amplitude is very strong. This did not stop Julie Snow from building, on the windswept rocks, a glass house cantilevered over the sea. A small building reduced to almost nothing in the immense landscape, it provides very generous views for the residents while also ensuring efficient protection on stormy days and during spring tides. Solid and well anchored on the rocks, this transparent house blends into the setting and lets itself be forgotten.

"The first time I came to this extraordinary, very uneven, and remote site with my client, we immediately identified, on the southeast part of the parcel, a finger of land going down toward the sea where it seemed possible to build a house," says the architect. "The rocky slope protected us from the west wind and, standing on a rocky crest, we discovered the sublime views offered by this site, of granite ground partially covered with low vegetation, facing the sea and the uninterrupted horizon line."

Julie Snow divided the program into two superposed and partially cantilevered parallelepipeds, secured to the ground by a stone wall. In search of an immaterial architecture, she wanted to make the façades a simple membrane by reducing as much as possible the thickness of the walls. As most of the walls were not load-bearing, the wood structure of the floors and the roof windbraced the house laterally so that it resists the force of even the strongest winds. The thickness of the floors and the roof is, in spite of it all, limited, to lessen the impact of the building.

As the construction site proved very difficult to access, the quality of work comes from the skills of local contractors. Apart from several visits to the construction site, the problems were mostly resolved by telephone, with photos used as backup.

On the interior, the spaces develop freely on two floors while accommodating the very tall areas, especially in the living room. Whether it is a reading room, living room, bedroom, or cantilevered terrace, each room benefits from a great diversity of vistas on the innumerable changes in the landscape.

The choice of materials and energy solutions responds to the constraints of the site. Made of glass, bluestone, galvanized steel, and wood, the exterior envelope is meant to withstand the assault by the ocean atmosphere. In winter, the high-performance thermal windows create a greenhouse effect, and in the region where the price of energy is relatively low, the heating works by a system of radiant panels built into the ceilings. To this is added an air exchange that brings in cool air in summer or when the house is unoccupied. With this vacation house, the owners periodically escape their hectic city lifestyle. The landscape is part of even their most insignificant activities, with the house forever slowing down the rituals of daily life.

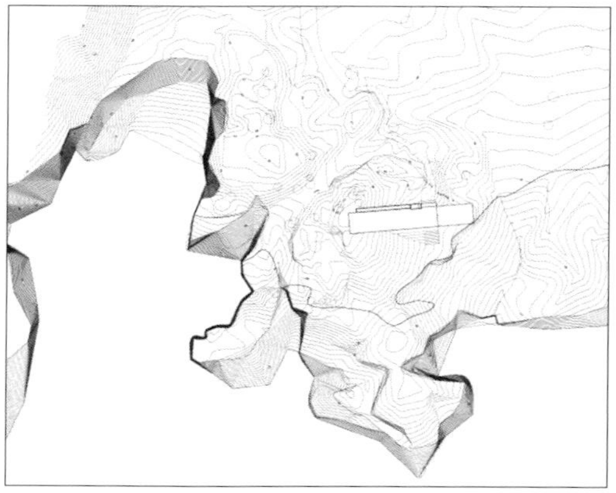

Location: Bay of Fundy, New Brunswick, Canada — Program: vacation house for a couple with two children, comprising two bedrooms and their bathrooms, a reading room, living room, kitchen, dining room, two outdoor platforms with terraces — Owners: David and Mary Beth Koehler — Architect: Julie Snow Architects — Technical consultants: Campbell Comeau Engineering Ltd., John Johnson Engineers, and Jack Snow Engineering — Surface area: 150 m^2 net living space — Cost of work: not disclosed — Schedule: completion, spring 2004 — Building system and materials: wood structure, aluminum joinery for the windows, dressed face of bluestone on concrete masonry, EPDM (Ethylene Propylene Diene Monomer) rubber on adhesive membrane, maplewood floors, concrete bathtub and sauna — General contractor: Erb Builders.

Set on the rocks in a landscape that is at once sublime, dramatic, and troubling, this refuge strives for immateriality.

The double-height living room. When they are indoors, the residents are always in contact with the ocean, even in the circulation spaces.

At the edge of the terrace, the wood floor and column are cantilevered compared with the corner.

Set on pilotis on uneven ground, the house is protected from bad weather by an edging on the roof. The structural columns are anchored in the granite. On the façade, windows alternate with solid sections of bluestone.

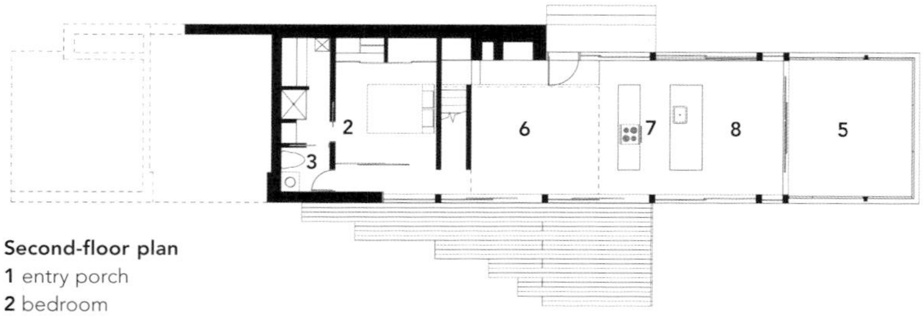

Second-floor plan
1 entry porch
2 bedroom
3 bathroom
4 reading room
5 platform
6 living room
7 kitchen
8 dining room

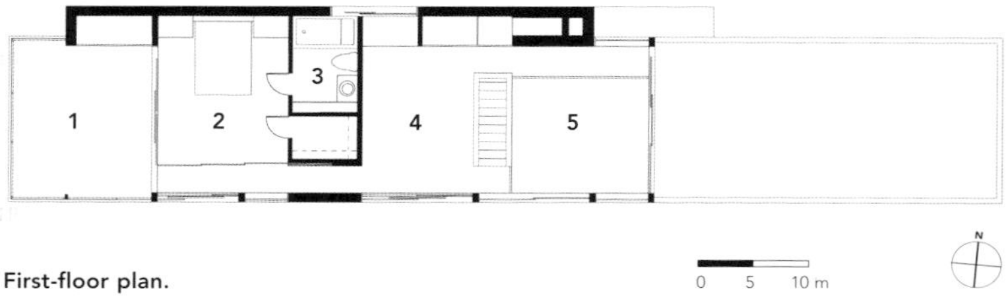

First-floor plan.

House on a Slope in Kobe, Japan

Shuhei Endo Architect Institute

On this uneven terrain in the Japanese archipelago, where the density of buildings is a crucial factor, the houses are often contorted to take advantage of inhospitable parcels that are assigned to them. In Kobe, this small, affordable house designed for a couple follows that very rule. Its architecture, inspired by the geometric folds of origami, clings to the steep slope of a site overhanging the railroad tracks facing Setonaikai, on the Inland Sea. The parcel is also edged by a Y-shaped intersection located at the foot of a hill, in a rather old residential area where houses are built on terraced land. This triangular site stretches over approximately 20 meters from east to west, with the width varying from 1.5 meters to 4 meters. To the north, in the rear, a cuneiform retaining wall of cut stone highlights a difference in height of 5 to 8 meters, depending on the area, compared with the reference ground.
Of course, the basic principle of this house rests on the idea of the ancient relationship between slopes and architecture. By drawing on the specificities of the location – the retaining wall and the modified ground – Shuhei Endo set about extending the characteristics of the setting to the architecture. Between the site and the frame, a reciprocal relationship of occupation is established. Thus the artificial components attach themselves to the slope so as to delineate a dynamic architecture in tension with the landscape.
The work involves a game of architectural additions resting on an artificial floor supported by five pillars, to which are added the walls and the roof, which closes off the space. The façade wall, which turns into the roof, is a sheet of metal siding with rectangular ridges. By folding and slanting, it adjusts itself to the topographical logic of the slope and of the triangular parcel. The alternation of open and closed spaces underscores the interaction with the site while also defining the spatial qualities of the house.
The setting, whether it be the sea, the talus with its stone wall, or the railroad infrastructure, can be seen from each room, which supports the unusual character of the house.
Access to the dwelling is from the top: the entrance leads to the living room, the bedroom, and the kitchen/dining area. All these rooms frame the sea while largely avoiding the view of the railroad tracks below. At this level, the roof and the floor that forms the artificial ground extend toward the north terrace to visually integrate the mineral retaining wall into the architecture. In the dining room, the view to the west is framed by the retaining wall and a new wall built to the south. The lower level has only an office, adjacent bathroom, and WC.

Location: Shoiya Tarumi-ku, Kobe, Japan — Program: affordable house for a couple, comprising a living room, a kitchen/dining area, a bedroom and bathroom, a home office, a small terrace — Owners: Ryosuke and Yasuko Unenishi — Architect: Shuhei Endo Architect Institute — Surface area: site, 130 m²; building, 50.3 m²; total floor area, 65.7 m² — Cost of work: 150,000 euros — Schedule: completion, March 2005 — Building system and materials: steel structure, galvanized steel siding used as the main material, parquet wood floors and plywood wall covering — Contractor: Sanwa Kensetsu Co.

In Japan, it is not unusual to build on odd parcels such as this one, situated above a railroad and facing the sea.

The architectural concept is based on the folding of a galvanized steel sheet that forms the façade and turns the corner for the roof.

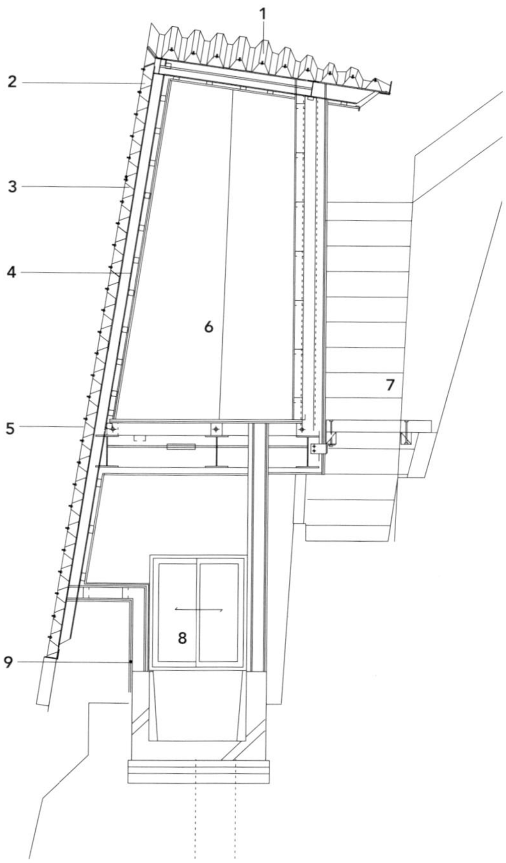

Cross section and detail of the siding
1 roof in undulating steel sheets
2 frame
3 galvanized steel (125 x 90 x 7 cm)
4 double windows (8 x 6 x 8 cm)
5 wall clad in undulating steel sheets
6 dining room
7 platform
8 bathroom
9 exterior wall in galvanized steel

View from the roof looking down on the railroad tracks.

The house creates its own artificial ground by attaching itself to the slope.

The retaining wall adds to the atmosphere of the place; between it and the rear of the house, a narrow platform was added to serve as a terrace.

The interior spaces seem to be in suspension. The bay windows make the environment very present: the retaining wall, the railroad, and the sea.

At the back of the kitchen, a narrow vertical window frames the view of the railroad and the Inland Sea.

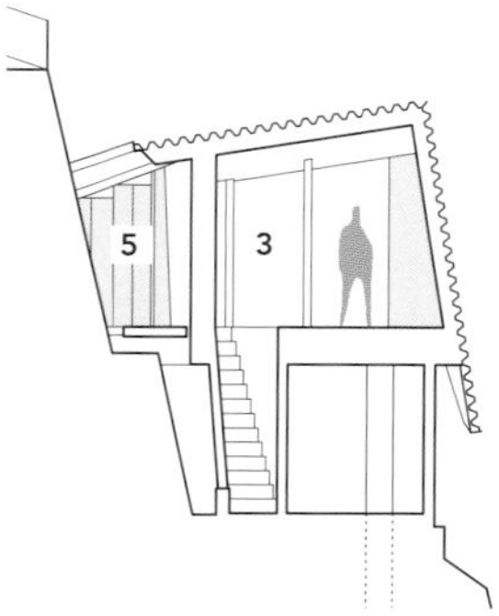

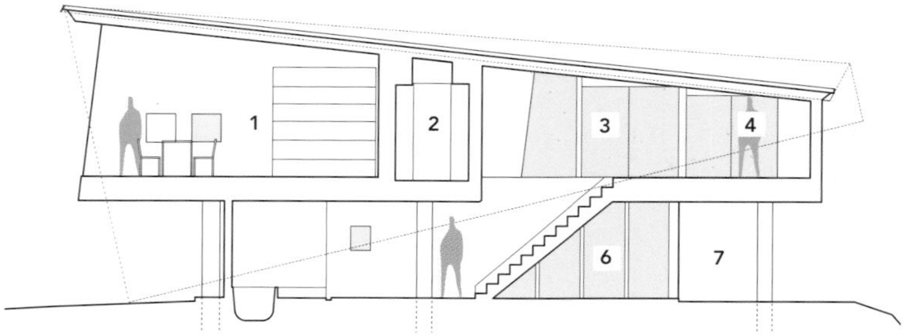

Cross section and longitudinal section.
1 kitchen/dining area
2 entrance
3 living room
4 bedroom
5 terrace
6 home office
7 courtyard

House on the Terraces in Sardinia, Italy

Antonio Citterio

To preserve the beauty of these coastal landscapes punctuated with rocky and sandy beaches, the Sardinian district of Villasimius created, all along the shore, a natural area where building is not allowed. The client, who owned a house there on approximately 40 hectares, amid grapevines and olive trees, asked Antonio Citterio to entirely restructure his house, taking advantage of a superb location. The original house dated to the 1970s.
With good southern exposure, it had a strange silhouette, complicated by a complex system of pergolas that the architects replaced with a flat roof, considerably reducing the impact of the building on the site. To the same end, they encircled the land around the house with unsquared-stone walls. By creating lines parallel to the horizon, the architects simplified the volume and clad the ground floor with a brown granite covering.
Thus the house springs up from the landscape with a new shape, which stands out simply in the setting. The pure forms and the alternation of solids and voids verge on abstraction.
The untreated materials attract the light while anchoring the architecture in the dry earth of Sardinia. "In this domesticated, partially planted nature, the house now appears like a detail," says the architect. Reduced to a white lime volume whose corners are softened by the intentionally imperfect handling of the plaster, this two-story building is also a luminous filter as well as an arrangement of frames. It finds shade thanks to the thickness of its envelope, but at the same time, the beveled embrasures enlarge the views.
Rather paradoxically, the creation of a retaining wall breaks down the boundaries between interior and exterior of the house, as between the immediate surroundings, the thirty or so hectares that surround the house, and the distant landscape.
A white prism emerges on the coast. The stone foundation blends with the outline of the walls of the patio, which gives the house an outdoor addition entirely in keeping with the interior space. The relationship to the sea, which is very close in spite of a height difference of nearly 3 meters, is handled by an identical stone wall. By naturally extending the design of the patio, where grapevines and olive trees are located, the wall gives the house suitable proportions.

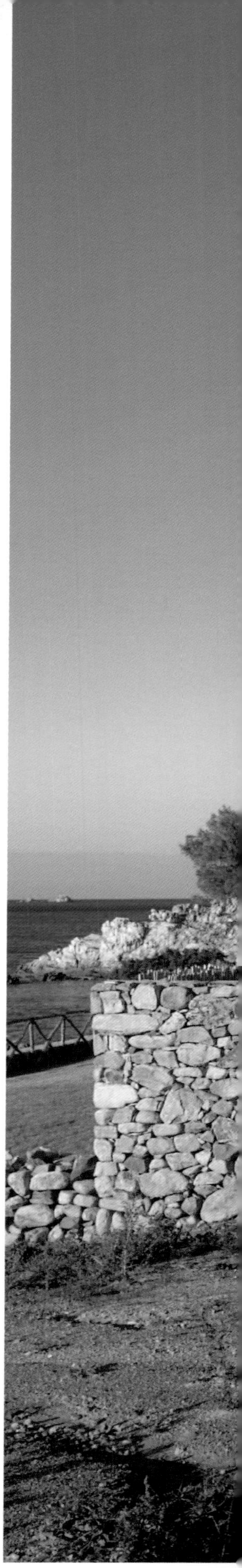

Location: Villasimius, Sardinia, Italy — Program: two-story single-family house with five bedrooms — Owner: private — Architect: Antonio Citterio — Surface area: land, 35 hectares; building, 450 m²; terrace, 300 m² — Cost of work: not disclosed — Schedule: design, 2003; completion, 2004 — Building system and materials: traditional masonry in concrete, stone, lime, basalt, granite, teak, insulated windows — Contractor: local artisans.

Long horizontal lines and untreated materials make the house blend into the landscape.

House on the Moor in Struer, Denmark

Jan Søndergaard

In southern Jutland in Denmark, the beauty of a landscape where the Nissum and Toftum fjords flow into the sea was a special source of inspiration for the artists of Denmark's golden age, in the nineteenth century. In the late 1930s, a painter, Jens Søndergaard, who lived on the very site of this house, painted many pictures, fascinated as he was by the light, the sky, and the reflections of a nature that he found "could not possibly be compared with God."

Jens Bang and his family owned a half kilometer of the coast and an old farm, away from everything; Bang asked the architect Jan Søndergaard to build a guest house for him. The heir to the famous Danish design company Bang Olufsen, he added that this house should be designed around the site, but also around a Philippe Starck bathtub that he had just purchased.

For the architect, to work on this untouchable site and "to capture" the sky in a unique space without disturbing the wild aspect of the hill was a challenge. The rudimentary architecture of the fishermen's huts spread out over the moor, with their single room surrounded by thick walls used for sleeping and storage, was for him a source of inspiration.

At the top of a desertlike dune that overlooks a prairie sloping down toward the coast, the house enjoys a panoramic view 200 degrees from east to west.

Its architecture comes down to two components: a concrete slab covered with a basalt floor and a copper shell. The slab constitutes a long continuous plane between the two terraces where one admires by turns the misty landscapes in the morning and the more contrasting landscapes of the evening. The copper shell forms the façade and turns back to form the roof. Closed toward the south slope, the shell opens to the east, west, and north, facing the Nissum Bredning coast.

The roof is punctured by a narrow longitudinal skylight that marks the separations between the secondary functions (shower, sink, kitchen, and WC), which are set in a secondary bar on the south façade, and the principal functions, arranged in the continuous open spaces facing the views. Along this spatial sequence, the functions are divided from east to west, and the activities seem to adapt themselves to the path of the sun: the bedroom faces the rising sun, then the bathroom, where the Starck bathtub is showcased by a long glazed façade, the living room, and finally, toward the setting sun, an office or meditation area containing among its unique furnishings a table and an enormous bookcase tucked into the service strip. Only three steel porticoes structure the building, with the roof and exterior walls made of prefabricated wood caissons. The exterior skin, specially designed by the architect with the contractor, is a simple sheet of very thin copper on standardized roofing paper.

To ensure the quality of the surface treatments, this flexible covering, slightly embossed owing to the compression of the materials, was cut into 0.80-by-1.2-centimeter units attached to the metal structure.

As it acquires a patina in the sea air, the facing take on a green color, in harmony with the vegetation.

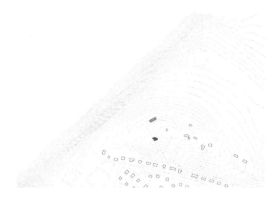

Location: Struer, Denmark — Program: house comprising a living room, bedroom, office/library, and a bathroom — Owner: Jens Bang — Architect: Jan Søndergaard, KHR arkitekter AS — Technical consultant for structure: Birch & Kroboe A/S v. Jesper Gath — Surface area: 141 m^2 net living space — Cost of work: 300,000 euros — Schedule: 2002-03 — Building system and materials: concrete, copper, and basalt — Contractor: Jens Bang Olufsen.

The abstract geometry of the house brings to mind the design of Bang Olufsen radios.

Poorly squared stone, lime rendering, basalt – the raw materials are fully in accord with the landscape.

Thick wood joinery and rare, carefully selected furniture – the ambience of the house borders on asceticism.

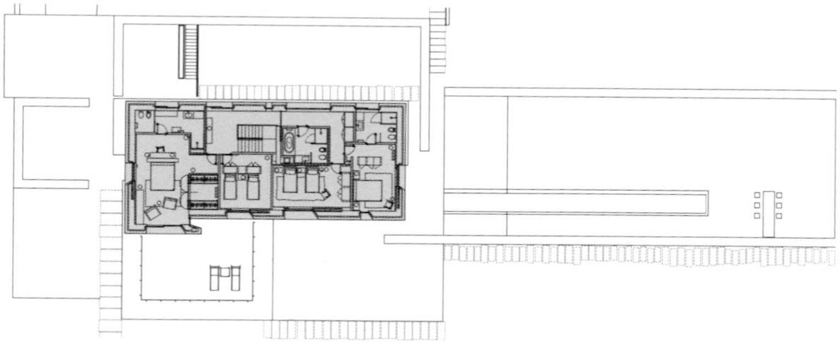

Upper-floor plan.

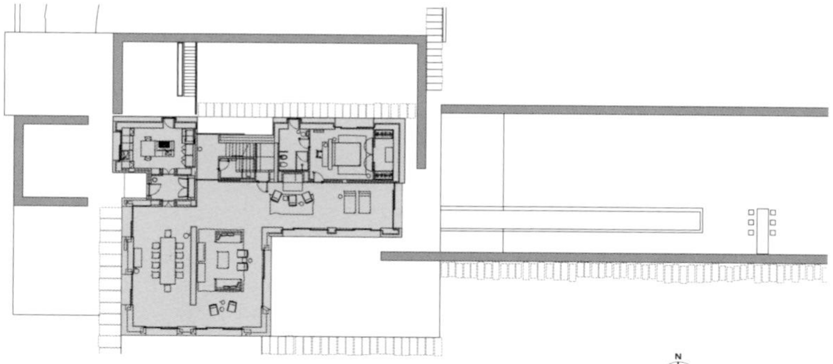

Ground-floor plan.

NATURAL MATERIALS AND THE TREATMENT OF DETAILS

All the materials are natural and biocompatible. Adapted to a coastal setting, the base rendering is obtained from a mixture of earth and fragments of brick and tiles that are ground up and then dried out. The rendering encourages the walls to breathe while also improving mechanical resistance. The rendering made from natural hydraulic lime is applied in two layers: when the first is dry, the surface is washed with water, then dabbed with a sponge to reveal the aggregate and its white hue.

The granite walls are approximately 20 centimeters thick, identical to the drystone walls that exist in the region.

Although great care has been taken with treatment of details, it is the rough appearance of the materials that predominates. The ground-floor terrace is paved with gray basalt slabs that are 8 centimeters thick; their uneven positioning lets the grass grow between them. Basalt is also used for the outdoor paths, the ground-level floors, and the staircase.

The interior rendering has a base of natural hydraulic lime, marble powder, and tinted earth with a smooth surface treatment achieved with a filling knife. In the kitchen and bathroom, the ochre and saffron rendering with a natural earth base is treated with beeswax.

House on the Moor in Struer, Denmark

Jan Søndergaard

In southern Jutland in Denmark, the beauty of a landscape where the Nissum and Toftum fjords flow into the sea was a special source of inspiration for the artists of Denmark's golden age, in the nineteenth century. In the late 1930s, a painter, Jens Søndergaard, who lived on the very site of this house, painted many pictures, fascinated as he was by the light, the sky, and the reflections of a nature that he found "could not possibly be compared with God."

Jens Bang and his family owned a half kilometer of the coast and an old farm, away from everything; Bang asked the architect Jan Søndergaard to build a guest house for him. The heir to the famous Danish design company Bang Olufsen, he added that this house should be designed around the site, but also around a Philippe Starck bathtub that he had just purchased.

For the architect, to work on this untouchable site and "to capture" the sky in a unique space without disturbing the wild aspect of the hill was a challenge. The rudimentary architecture of the fishermen's huts spread out over the moor, with their single room surrounded by thick walls used for sleeping and storage, was for him a source of inspiration.

At the top of a desertlike dune that overlooks a prairie sloping down toward the coast, the house enjoys a panoramic view 200 degrees from east to west.

Its architecture comes down to two components: a concrete slab covered with a basalt floor and a copper shell. The slab constitutes a long continuous plane between the two terraces where one admires by turns the misty landscapes in the morning and the more contrasting landscapes of the evening. The copper shell forms the façade and turns back to form the roof. Closed toward the south slope, the shell opens to the east, west, and north, facing the Nissum Bredning coast.

The roof is punctured by a narrow longitudinal skylight that marks the separations between the secondary functions (shower, sink, kitchen, and WC), which are set in a secondary bar on the south façade, and the principal functions, arranged in the continuous open spaces facing the views. Along this spatial sequence, the functions are divided from east to west, and the activities seem to adapt themselves to the path of the sun: the bedroom faces the rising sun, then the bathroom, where the Starck bathtub is showcased by a long glazed façade, the living room, and finally, toward the setting sun, an office or meditation area containing among its unique furnishings a table and an enormous bookcase tucked into the service strip. Only three steel porticoes structure the building, with the roof and exterior walls made of prefabricated wood caissons. The exterior skin, specially designed by the architect with the contractor, is a simple sheet of very thin copper on standardized roofing paper.

To ensure the quality of the surface treatments, this flexible covering, slightly embossed owing to the compression of the materials, was cut into 0.80-by-1.2-centimeter units attached to the metal structure.

As it acquires a patina in the sea air, the facing take on a green color, in harmony with the vegetation.

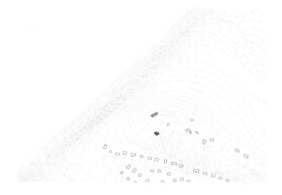

Location: Struer, Denmark — Program: house comprising a living room, bedroom, office/library, and a bathroom — Owner: Jens Bang — Architect: Jan Søndergaard, KHR arkitekter AS — Technical consultant for structure: Birch & Kroboe A/S v. Jesper Gath — Surface area: 141 m^2 net living space — Cost of work: 300,000 euros — Schedule: 2002-03 — Building system and materials: concrete, copper, and basalt — Contractor: Jens Bang Olufsen.

The abstract geometry of the house brings to mind the design of Bang Olufsen radios.

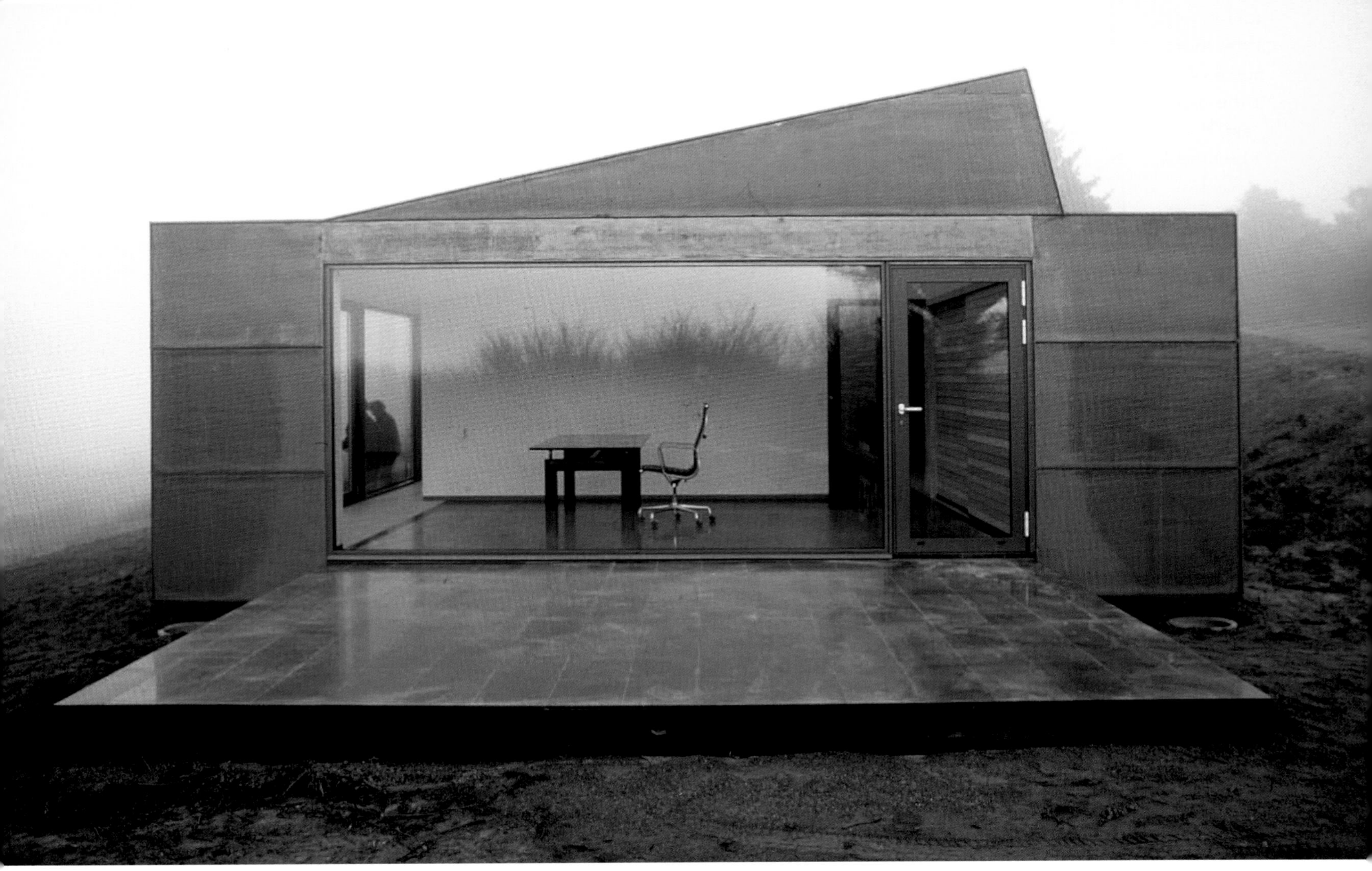

The paved surface at the doorway extends to the interior of the house before spilling out onto the opposite terrace.

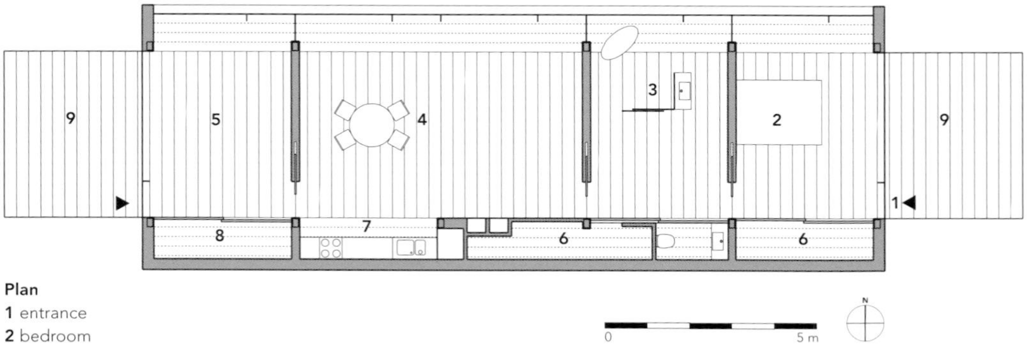

Plan
1 entrance
2 bedroom
3 bathroom
4 living/dining area
5 office
6 storage
7 kitchen
8 library
9 terrace

The office, at the western end of the house, is wide open to the sea. The indoor flooring extends onto the terrace.

In this harsh and very windy climate, bay windows with high-quality glass provide good insulation.

Wood-fired heating is provided by very long radiators inserted in the floor, along the windows.

The Philippe Starck bathtub, playing a leading role in the space.

Bastion House in Coliumo, Chile

Mauricio Pezo and Sofia von Ellrichshausen

On the Coliumo Peninsula, 550 kilometers from Santiago, the house sits on a semideserted cliff facing the Pacific Ocean. This concrete cube punctured with square openings transforms itself according to its successive uses. By turns a vacation house and a setting for seminars, it is also an art gallery and cultural center, in a rural area inhabited by farmers and fishermen and frequented by only a few tourists. Through its simplicity, it stands – and stands out – as a solitary entity in a sublime and desolate landscape.

Deliberately avoiding any mimicry of the landscape and any borrowing of seaside housing typologies, the architects opted for a compact volume that preserves the appearance of a natural promontory surrounded by vast expanses and the unforgettable view at the base of the cliffs. The double function influences the appearance of this informal place. Both public and private, monumental and domestic, the Casa Poli nevertheless avoids the negative effects of such ambiguity of use.

The linchpin of the project is the double thickness of the façades, which frees up the central space for multiple activities. Beyond its thermal role, it brings together the vertical circulation routes leading up to the roof terrace, the kitchens and bathrooms, the closets and interior balconies protected from the sun and rain.

All the domestic objects, easily stashed, disappear without any fuss when the picture rails are needed during exhibitions.

On the interior, three platforms zigzag from the ground floor to the terrace with variations in level. The logic of the square openings is extended, marking the successive planes and a play of perspectives that reinforces the double envelope. The skillful arrangement of openings and frames with precise viewpoints and the raised floor help turn the sea, vertiginous at the foot of the cliffs, into a scenograph. The gaze sometimes turns outward or, in a more introverted way, toward the interstitial void and toward the triple-height studio around which the staircases are arranged.

To build at the edge of the world meant making due with local labor, with all of four wheelbarrows and a concrete mixer. Everything was poured in place using the untreated wood casings in horizontal layers of a height equal to half the casing. Recycled on the interior, the wood casing forms the components of the partition and sliding panels that close off the openings on the perimeters – the gallery function means avoiding large bays – and serve as security shutters when the house is not occupied.

Spartan and modest in terms of its budget, the Casa Poli expresses the drama of a modern bastion, on the edge of a cliff facing the ocean.

Location: Coliumo Peninsula, Chile — Program: house that serves alternatively as a summer residence, a cultural center, and an exhibition gallery, comprising several adaptable spaces, a large studio, bedrooms, kitchens, and bathrooms — Owners: Eduardo Meissner and Rosmarie Prim (Casa Poli Cultural Center) — Architects: Mauricio Pezo and Sofia von Ellrichshausen — Technical consultant for structure: Cecilia Poblete — Surface area: site, 10,000 m^2; building, 180 m^2 net living space — Cost of work: 52,000 euros. — Schedule: design, 2002-03; construction, 2003-05 — Building system: concrete structure — Contractor: PvE.

The thickness of the double façade creates an unusual image at the top of the cliff.

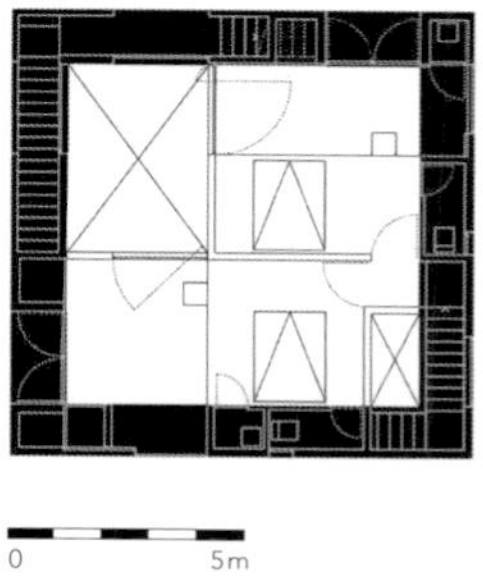

Plan of the spaces fit between the two envelopes.

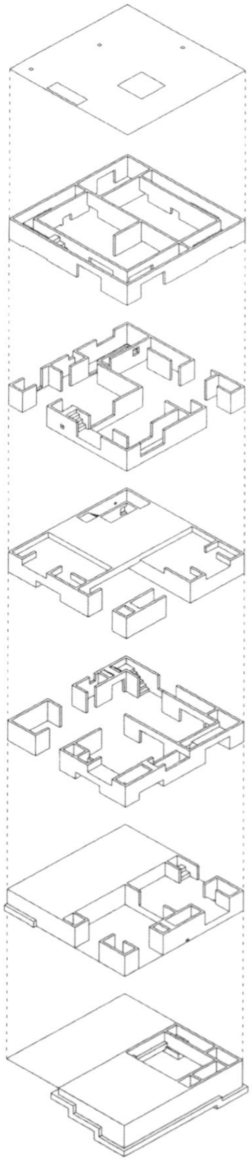

Axonometric view of the various levels.

Shelter or vertigo: Throughout the architectural promenade, one's impressions change. At right, the triple-height living room/studio.

The space between, for circulation and service areas.

The space between provides depth and successive planes. Articulating the interior spaces, the same square openings are found on the façade.

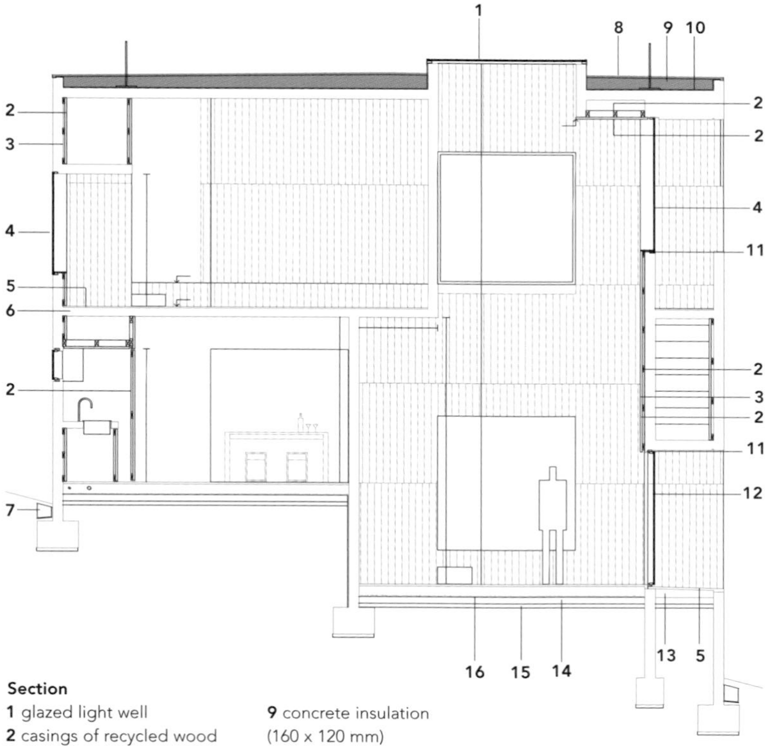

On the interior, partitions, doors, and shutters of concrete wood were painted white. Their appearance goes well with the rough concrete.

The setting for a vacation resort, for art exhibitions, and for seminars, the Casa Poli reconciles its many functions though great diversity in its spaces and circulation patterns.

Section
1 glazed light well
2 casings of recycled wood
3 polystyrene thermal insulation (30 mm)
4 fixed double glazing
5 mortar bed (30 mm)
6 floor slab (140 mm)
7 drainage system (300 mm)
8 mortar bed with an impermeable cover (30 mm)
9 concrete insulation (160 x 120 mm)
10 tarred layer (5 mm)
11 aluminum frame
12 double-glazed door to the balcony
13 reinforced-concrete slabs (140 mm)
14 gravel bed (10 mm)
15 reinforced floor (60 mm)
16 waterproofing (5 mm)

2

The House at the Water's Edge

4 x 4 House in Kobe, Japan

Tadao Ando

This Kobe Bay house, which belongs to the head of a construction company, faces Japan's Inland Sea. "It is a sensitive environment subject to marine erosion. A large part of the site was already transformed into an unusually beautiful sand beach, with a strip of dry land preserved behind a water gate," explains the architect. On the opposite bank, 4 kilometers away, lies Awaji Island, where the city of Hokudai was the epicenter of the earthquake in 1995. To the east, the Akashi Strait bridge, the largest suspension bridge in the world and the linchpin for the development of the port of Kobe, stretches into the landscape. This site made it possible for Tadao Ando to develop his thoughts on the relationship between man and the natural elements through a spatial experience; at the same time, he turned once again to Awaji Island, where he had already built a water temple and the Yumebutai Conference Center. Another challenge: opening a dialogue with the immense structure of the Akashi bridge, "a real show of technological know-how by Japanese builders."

A small minimalist tower, four stories high, on a square plan of 4 meters per side, the house echoes the installations in the port and the surrounding residences. Relatively closed on the ground floor, where only a French window in the hall opens onto the sea, it is crowned on the upper part by a transparent double-height cube that features a space suspended between the sky and the water. This volume, cantilevered toward the sea, is pushed out one meter beyond the east face of the building in order to make room on the interior for a side staircase.

"This cube frames a panorama that encompasses the whole extent of the Inland Sea, Awaji Island, and the Akashi bridge, where, for the owner of the house and for me, the memories of the earthquake are embedded," said Tadao Ando. "Long after completing this house, I dreamed of expanding it toward the sea, knowing that it would half disappear with the high tide."

In the bedroom on the second floor, the views are carefully framed by a vertical French window on the south and a small square window on the east; above, the office is open on three sides.

With a structural system of reinforced-concrete walls, the house rests on a basement that was thoroughly researched so that all the construction details and structural reinforcements meet the antiseismic and erosion-control requirements. To mitigate the alterations linked to salt and seawater, the distance between the steel reinforcing rods and the concrete surface was set at 40 millimeters. The concrete skin was then covered with a painted fluoroethylene resin. The composition of the concrete itself was adapted to the setting: it is a very hard concrete in which the quantity of water used is less than in the usual ratios.

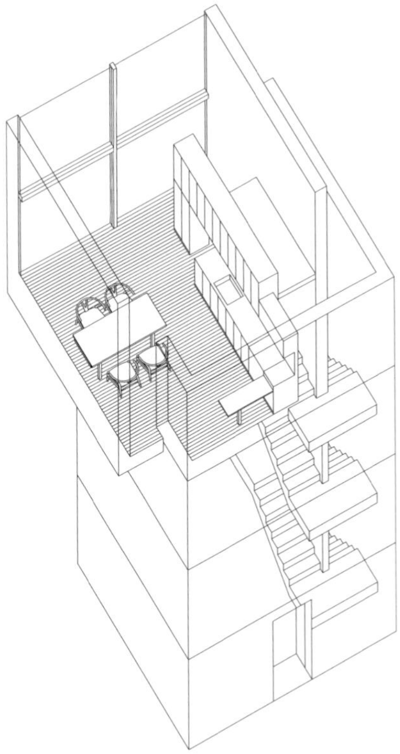

Location: port of Kobe, Japan — Program: residence on four levels, with one room per floor (bathroom and WC, bedroom, office, living room with an integrated kitchen nook) — Owner: Nakata Construction Company — Architect: Tadao Ando — Surface area: site, 65 m²; building, 23 m²; total floor area, 118 m² — Cost of work: not disclosed — Schedule: design, April 2001 – April 2002; construction, August 2002 – February 2003 — Building system: concrete shell structure and antiseismic basement — General contractor: Nakata Construction Company.

This little four-story tower topped with a transparent cube evokes the verticality of lighthouses and observation posts.

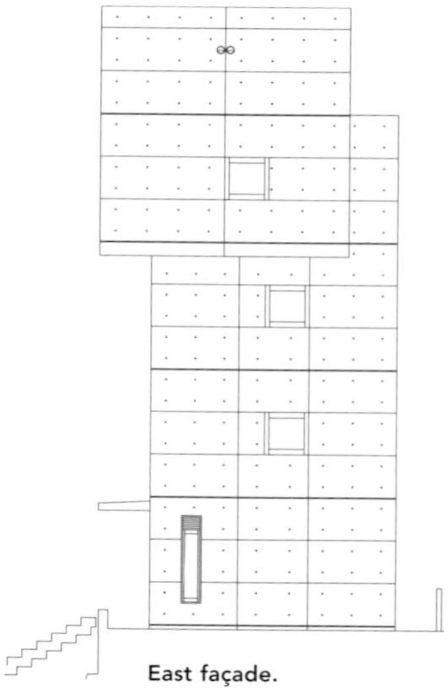

East façade.

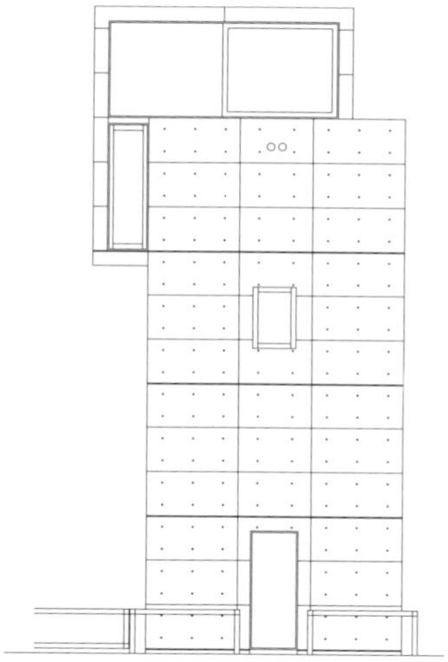

North façade.

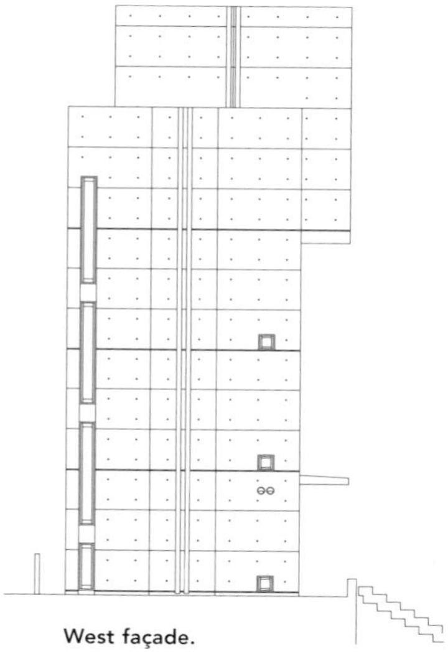

West façade.

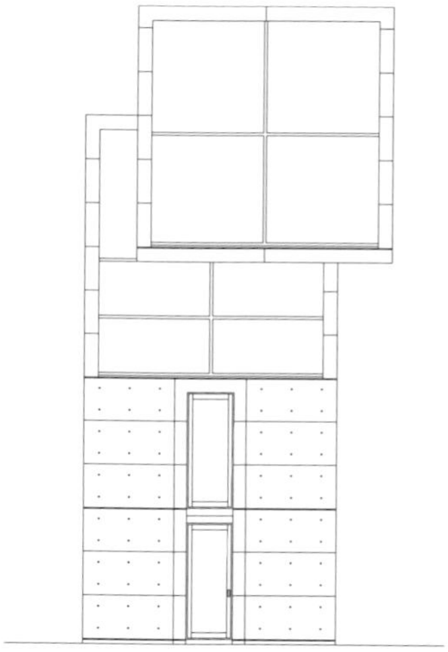

South façade.

0 5m

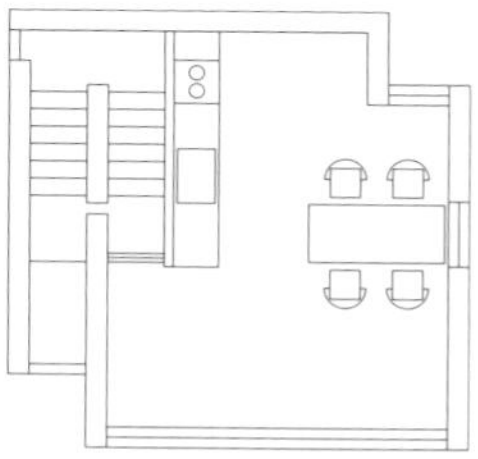

Fourth-floor plan, with the living room and kitchen nook.

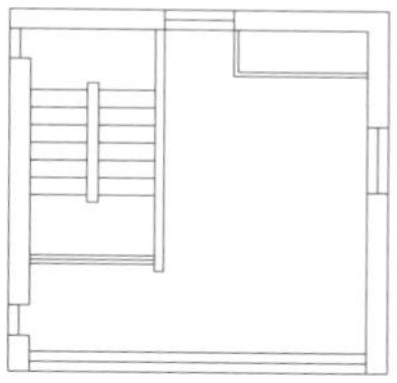

Third-floor plan, with the office.

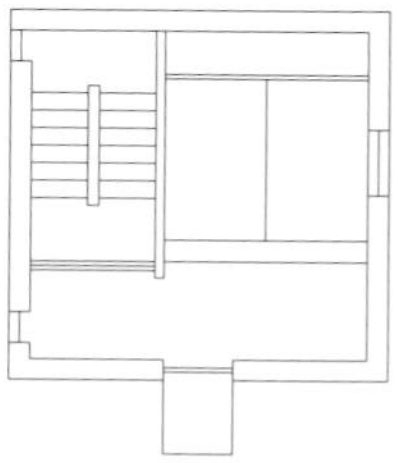

Second-floor plan, with the bedroom.

First-floor plan, with the bathroom and WC.

The living room on the top floor.

A dialogue with the landscape, near or far, and with the Akashi bridge.

The materiality of the concrete reinforces the framing.

A geometric house in a shifting environment.

Floating House in Kalmar, Sweden

Staffan Strindberg

"To live in contact with the water and with nature awakens the senses," says architect Staffan Strindberg. "We wanted to convey the sense that the water was entering the living room. With the light come the reflections, a bit like in the houses that line the Bosporus in Istanbul. Owing to the sound and the smell of the water, one experiences a sensation of freedom."

The client runs Tecomatic, a firm specializing in the construction of underwater concrete structures. Together, architect and client studied the concept of a floating house, without a precise location but with the idea of being able to have several such houses on one site and to take advantage of the interior spaces by organizing a double orientation, a private one toward the water and a public one on the quay side.

Does a floating house have to look like a boat? For the architect, "It is not at all like a boat, but rather like a living unit that takes the environment into account by opening to the outdoors." Though the house is intended to remain at the same site for a long time, indeed permanently, the architect nevertheless took pains to make it easy to transport.

As modern conveniences and stability were essential, he responded with a square plan that concentrated the functions on two floors topped by a terrace with a garden and its own kitchenette. "The square is a simple shape that brings a feeling of calm to take advantage of the view of the water, and the central staircase brings the relationship outdoors." The entrance is wedged at wharf level; the kitchen is adjacent to it and, together with the living room and the terrace, forms an enormous two-story open space; finally, the living room and the master bedroom are as close to the water as possible.

When the town of Kalmar became interested in the project, it made available to the designers a site that was a former navy yard on the port, in the center of town. Echoing the fishermen's houses on the nearby Ängö Island, the façade is in traditional Swedish red.

With a humid and very cold climate where the wind, snow, and ice required specific materials and technical solutions, the durability of the structure, its stability on the water, and its thermal balance were crucial. To be able to use all the materials on the interior without any restrictions, the architect created an insulating envelope. A heavy concrete shell designed with K-V Bygg ensures stability.

The structure is waterproofed and insulated using a light sandwich-partition, gelled on the exterior and clad on the inner side with gypsum panel; between the two, there is an insulation void. Apart from regularly oiled wood, the chosen materials – glass, lacquered aluminum, and stainless steel – minimize upkeep. Although the house has no cold bridge, and despite the chilly temperatures, electricity consumption for heating remains under 9,000 kilowatt hours per year. The house has floor heating, fed with a heat pump that draws water from the port. Before discharging the polluted air, the heat is taken back into the system.

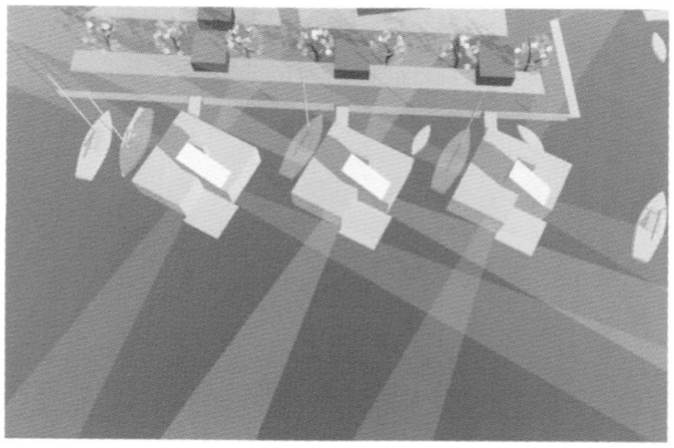

Location: Kalmar, Sweden — Program: floating house, 12 x 12 m, comprising a kitchen, dining room, living room, office, three bedrooms, two bathrooms, a laundry area, and two terraces, one with a kitchenette — Owner: private — Architect: Staffan Strindberg — Surface area: building, 178 m^2 net living space; terraces, 25 m^2 and 75 m^2 — Cost of work: 570,000 euros — Schedule: 2002-03 — Building system and materials: total weight, 165 tons; depth in the water, 1.3 m; 74 m^2 of glazing — Contractors: general contractor, Tecomatic; shell and insulation, K-V Bygg.

General view of the house. It is attached to a general electricity distribution network, as required by the town.

Sections.

This floating house was nominated Building of the Year for 2003 by the Swedish Building Industries Prize. Since then, the architect has made use of this concept of the floating house with a square plan, varying the scale.

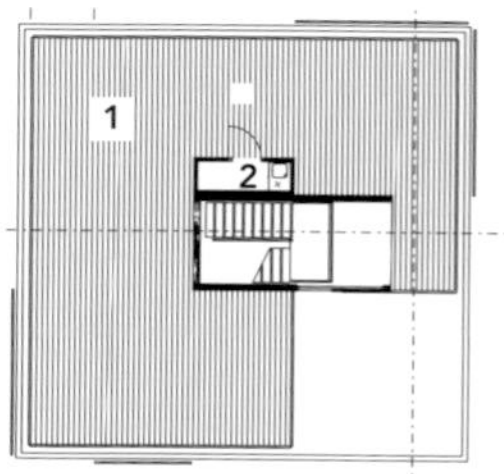

Roof plan
1 terrace
2 kitchenette

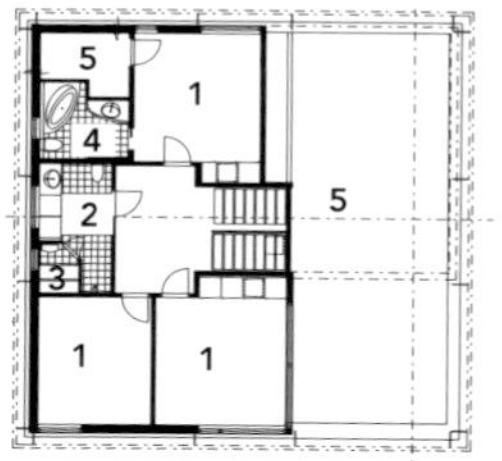

Upper-floor plan
1 bedroom
2 bathroom and laundry area
3 sauna
4 bathroom
5 equipment room
6 storage

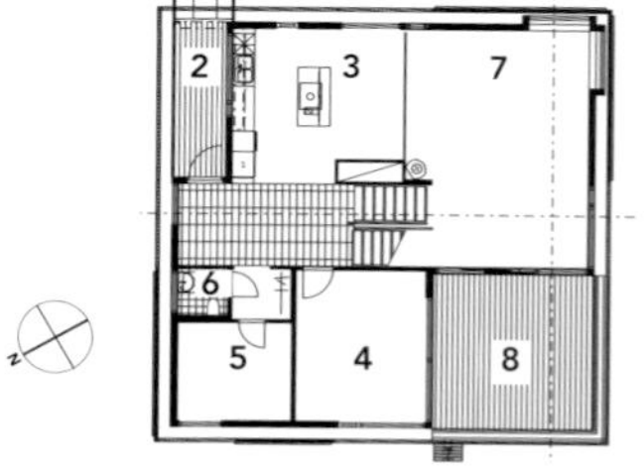

Entry-level plan
1 walkway
2 entrance
3 kitchen
4 dining room
5 office
6 WC
7 living room
8 terrace

0 5 10 m

A FEW WORDS FROM THE ARCHITECT ON COMMERCIALIZATION AND THE LEGAL FRAMEWORK

"This project goes beyond my usual concerns as an architect. My client had long dreamed of a floating house. Before we met, he had seen various designs for covered boats rejected by the town. To take it a step further, he contacted K-V Bygg, a company I had previously worked with for the Swedish Environment Agency. We then decided to expand the concept and commercialize it by setting up a special-purpose company. Two issues still had to be resolved: the grouping together of houses and their legal integration into the town. The fact that the town accepted the design was a major impetus. The town recognized that the water, in itself, could constitute a 'site,' whereas the law stipulated that 'any residence had to be built on solid ground.' It was therefore necessary to find a legal framework. Thus Kalmar became the first Swedish town (and, no doubt, the first town in the North) to plan a floating settlement within the framework of existing urban regulations. For the municipality, our concept helped make this town a pleasant living environment."

House with a Prow in Essex, New York, USA

Steven Holl

In a dialogue with the site that rarely excludes metaphor and poetry, the New York architect Steven Holl begins his designs with abstract compositions. Near the U.S.-Canadian border, on the banks of Lake Champlain, which is often compared to an inland sea, this house is no exception. With its distorted prow, it resembles a strange, laminated copper vessel, anchored for a long stopover. Through a formal game, the contours of the plan and those of the façades are almost identical. Attached to a wooden framework, the copper cladding gives a patina to the house, which completely blends with the vegetation each fall. Accessible by boat, the house fits discreetly with the stonework lining the bank. The copper reflections allude to the industrial heritage of the village.
With a series of geometrical openings that introduce natural light and punctuate the route, this building is in the tradition of an office building constructed by the architect along a canal in Amsterdam in 2000. Here, twenty-four windows punctuate the façade. This number corresponds to the number of chapters in Homer's *Odyssey*, from which Holl drew inspiration, entranced by the idea of an imaginary voyage that ends on the site of a former nail factory on the outskirts of the town of Essex. Intrigued by the past of this nineteenth-century industrial town, the owner is himself a collector of nails.
The spareness of the exterior contrasts sharply with the dynamic lift of the interior, where the spaces unfold in a spiral, bathed in light from the windows and sustained by their rhythm. The northwest façade is completely opaque; the openings are spread unequally on the other three sides: fourteen on the northeast, five on the southeast, and another five on the southwest.
The four-story unit features an irregular lozenge-shaped plan, accommodating an empty space running up and down behind the north façade. Above the basement level, which is allocated for storage, the first floor houses the entrance, double-height living room, kitchen, and bathroom. The library and a studio occupy the second floor, and the third is given over to a loft. The white plaster walls are warmed by parquet floors and wood furniture, wall shelving, and built-in modular bookcases… On the interior, the range of materials confers great simplicity.
The handling of voids and solids creates views from one room to the next. When the cut of the windows frames the waterscape like a series of photographs, the prevailing atmosphere in the house is at once calm and playful.

Location: Essex, New York, USA — Program: residence comprising a living room, kitchen, bathroom, library and studio, a loft, and a storeroom — Owner: private — Architect: Steven Holl Architects — Surface area: 109 m² net living space — Cost of work: not disclosed — Schedule: 2002-04 — Building system and materials: concrete structure; concrete retaining walls on the bank; wooden beams; exterior walls: wood frame, plywood veneer, polyethelene vapor barrier, Tyvek membrane, copper sheet siding; roof: wood joists, plywood roof cladding, polymer membrane, drainage for the roof and gutters; structure and exterior staircases in metal, railing and hardware in steel; interior ceiling and wall surfacing in gypsum panels covered with a skin of white plaster of the same thickness; floors of the studio, loft, and ground floor in wood boards; floors of the kitchen and the bathroom in local stone; interior staircases in ash; surfacing of the basement in plywood with organic asphalt — Contractor: not disclosed.

Turning toward the water, the prow shows the verticality of an unusual metal prism that sparkles in the sun.

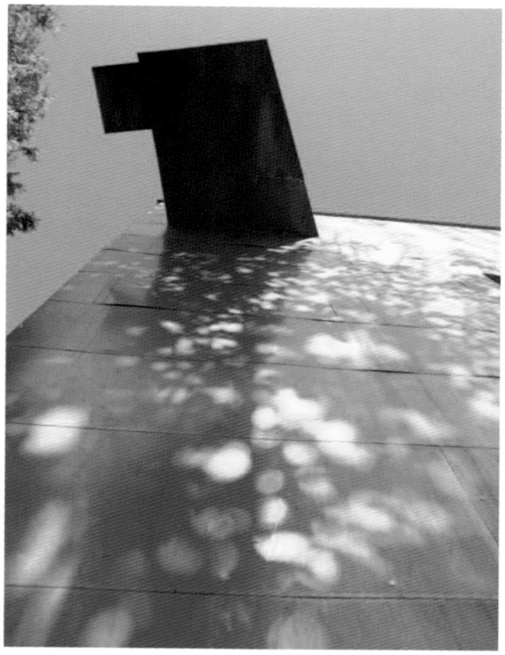

With twenty-four windows on three façades, the house is clad in a skin of laminated copper sheets.

The belvedere, at the top. The shadows of the foliage are reflected on the copper facing, which reflects the light.

On the interior, built-in shelving frees up the space.

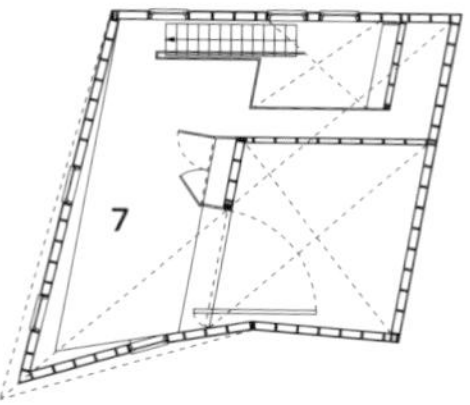

Top-floor plan.

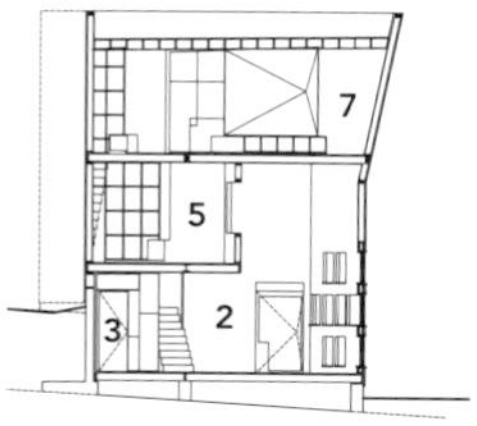

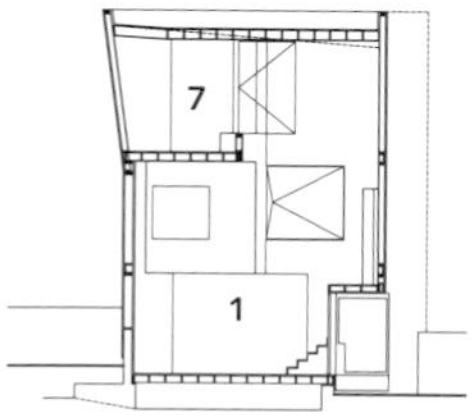

Sections.

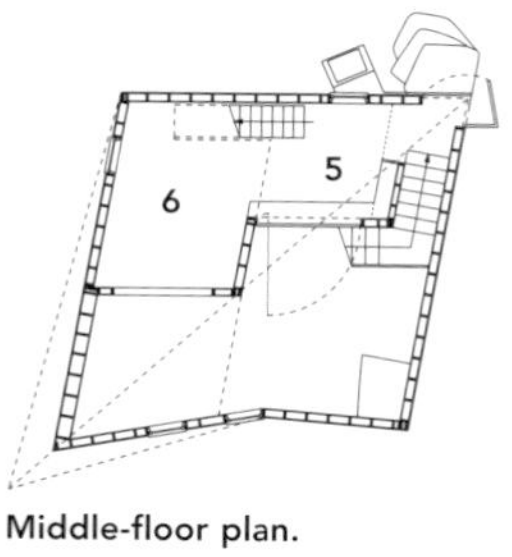

Middle-floor plan.

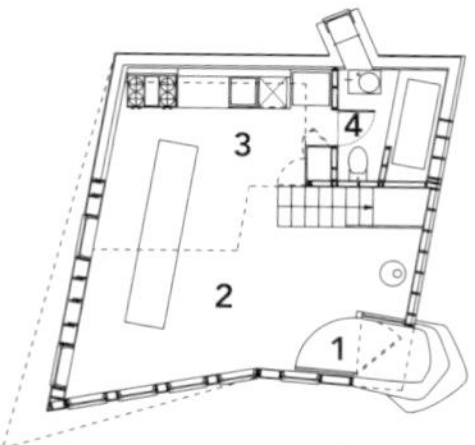

Ground-floor plan.

1 entrance
2 living room
3 kitchen
4 bathroom
5 library
6 studio
7 loft

0 5 10 m

N

On the interior, a light, delicate spiral staircase offers access to the living room.

The bathroom, facing the oyster farm.

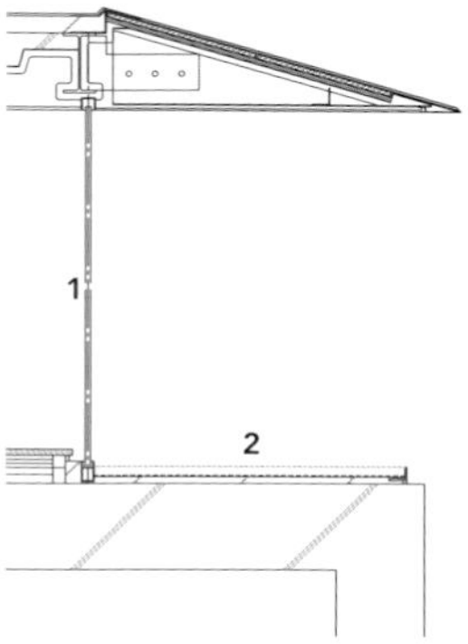

Detail, section through the terrace, sheltered by the roof overhang
1 bay window
2 water

On the terrace, the plane of water visually extends the surface of the ocean. The outdoor columns are made of galvanized steel. The detail on the carefully handled windows and the delicacy of the joinery emphasize visual continuity.

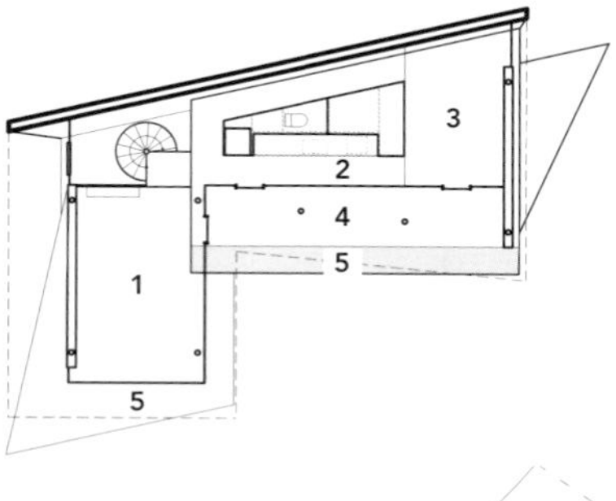

Upper-floor plan
1 living/dining area
2 kitchen
3 master bedroom
4 terrace
5 water

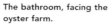

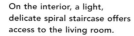

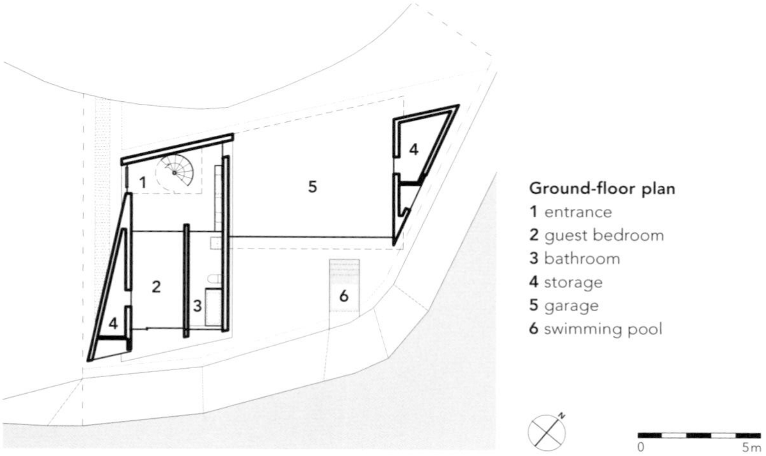

Ground-floor plan
1 entrance
2 guest bedroom
3 bathroom
4 storage
5 garage
6 swimming pool

Origami House in Hatsukaichi, Japan

Katsufumi Kubota

With its glass walls and its large concrete walls folded back to welcome the sea, this house is a privileged observation spot on Japan's Inland Sea, opposite Miyajima Island, to the west of Hiroshima. The site, one of few available for residential use in the area, borders a curved street that has a panoramic view of the water. The plan adjusts to the arc of the parcel by two triangular recesses. At high tide, the slight difference in level between sea and land – only 4 meters – truly gives the impression that the parcel is floating on the water. At low tide, the water drops 2 meters, revealing a bed of sand and the lines of an oyster farm.

"When we design a project, we begin by observing the context and taking advantage of the topography and the spirit of the place to open a dialogue. Here, the image of a sheet of paper rocking in the waves came to us, and this dictated the concept. A concrete slab folds over toward the bank to grab the sea. It defines the envelope of the house, which is closed on the street façade to avoid the gazes of passersby," explains the architect. Painted white, reinforced and wind-braced by a steel frame, the house rests on a concrete structure. Steel components covered with cement and a layer of waterproof urethane support the angle of the roof, whose aerodynamic shape helps deflect the wind, which sometimes blows at more than 50 meters per second. A narrow door, more than 5 meters high, marks the street entrance.

The terrace and its ornamental pool constitute one of the most attractive areas of the house. The white reflects the light of the sun, and the sharp corner of the roof visually lightens its weight while also cutting into the blue of the sky.

On the interior, a spiral staircase leads to the upper level, which is inundated with light. With some vertical areas, some sloping areas, and some horizontal areas resulting from the shape of the envelope, the interior is characterized by the variety of its mostly glazed spaces, to which the architect did not wish to assign a fixed use. The upstairs bedroom can thus serve as a dining room, and when not in use, the guest bedroom on the ground floor can become a hall. On the floor, latex coverings and ash floorboards provide pleasing contact for bare feet. With a skillful layout that stimulates the senses and puts one in touch with the elements, the house captures the fleeting fluctuations of the landscape.

"Beyond its sculptural and minimalist image, the luxury of the house lies above all in the natural setting. The sunlight and clouds, the waves and flashes of lightning, the wind, the smells and sounds, even down to the flight of migrating birds – these are essential parts in the spatial experience."

Location: Hatsukaichi, Hiroshima, Japan — Program: two-story house with swimming pool, garage, and terrace, comprising a living/dining area, kitchen, two bedrooms, and a bathroom — Owner: private — Architect: Kubota Architect Atelier, Katsufumi Kubota, architect — Surface area: 154.23 m^2 net living space — Cost of work: not disclosed — Schedule: design, April 2001 – June 2003; construction, September 2003 – July 2004 — Building system and materials: combined structure of reinforced concrete and steel, and cement mortar — General contractor: Nomura Construction.

At the entrance, on the north façade, is a narrow door, 5.35 meters tall and 0.90 meters wide.

Opaque on the side facing the town, the house chooses its views of the immediate surroundings.

The massing of the house delineates a sheltered porch. As it folds, the white-painted concrete curtain creates, at human scale, a protective screen facing the horizon.

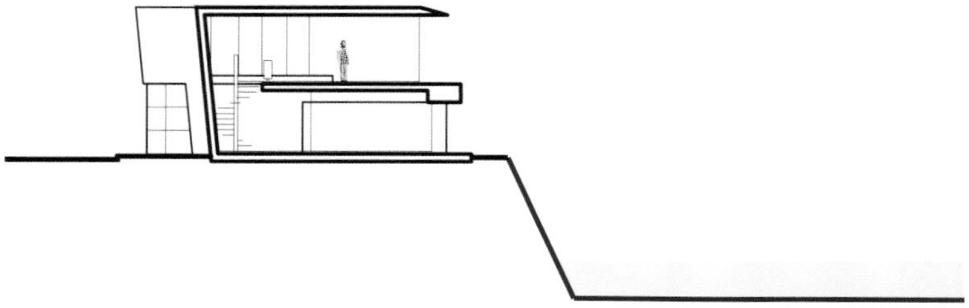

The movement of the tides creates different sensations, depending on the time of day.

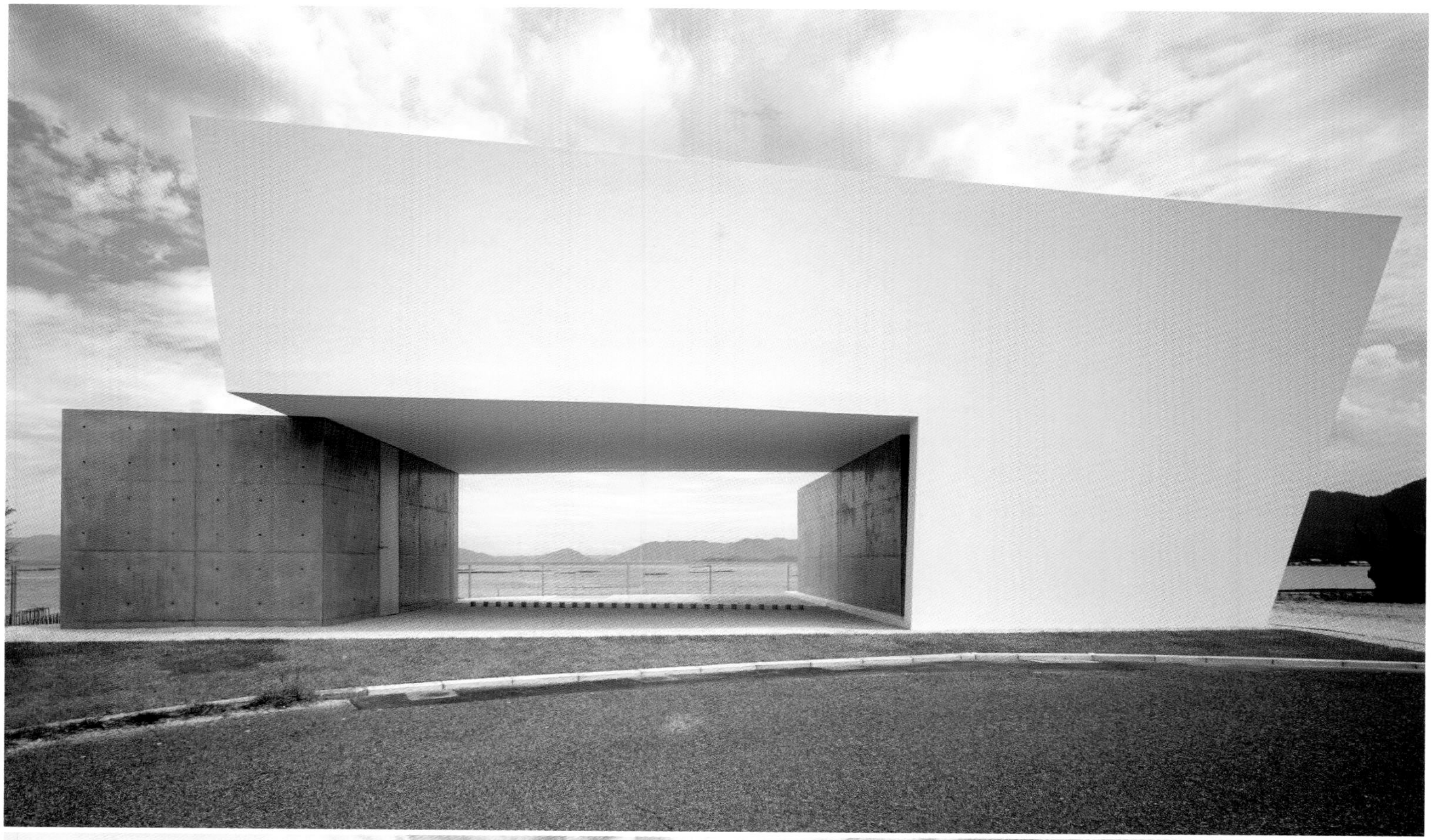

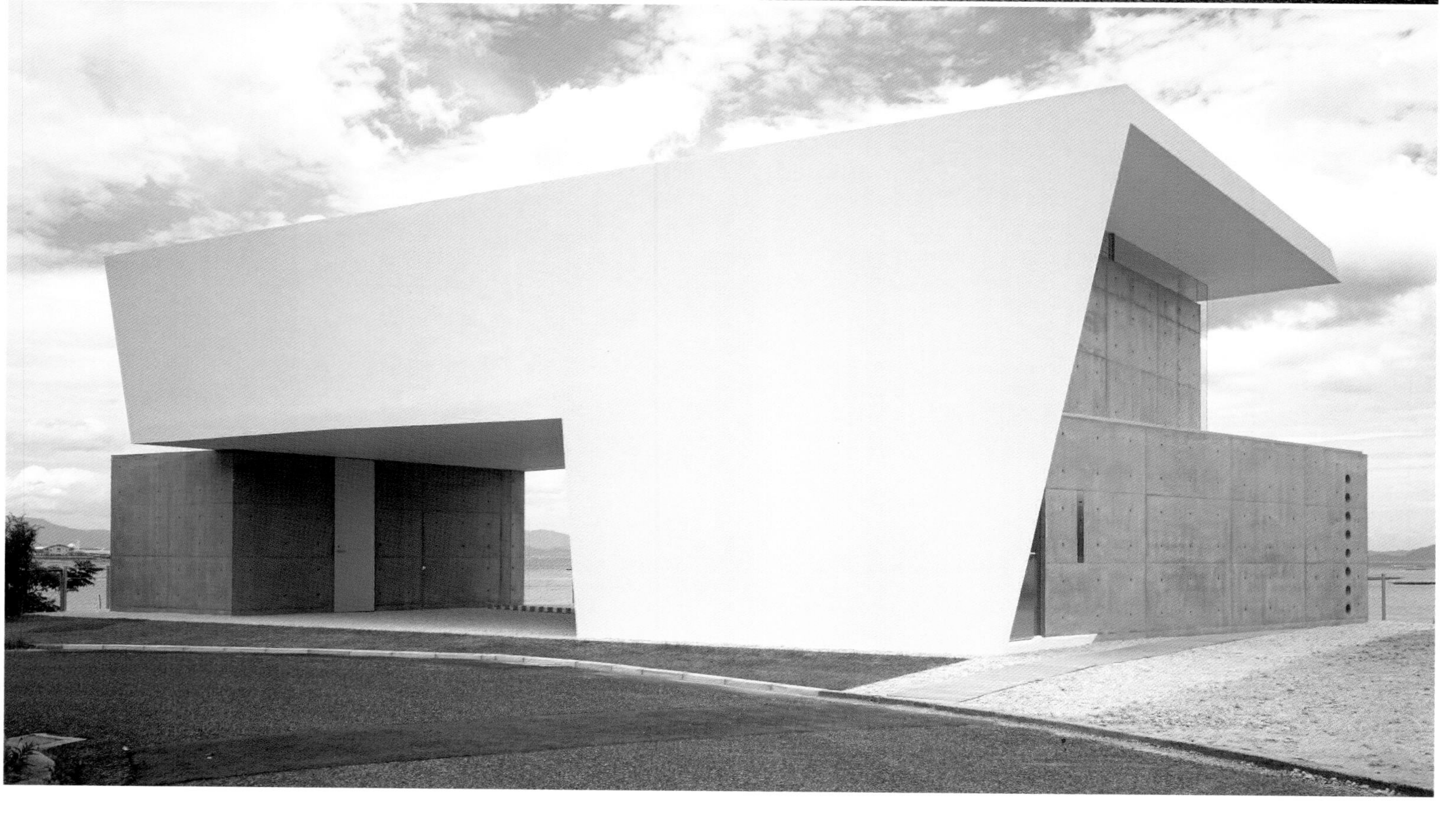

On the interior, a light, delicate spiral staircase offers access to the living room.

The bathroom, facing the oyster farm.

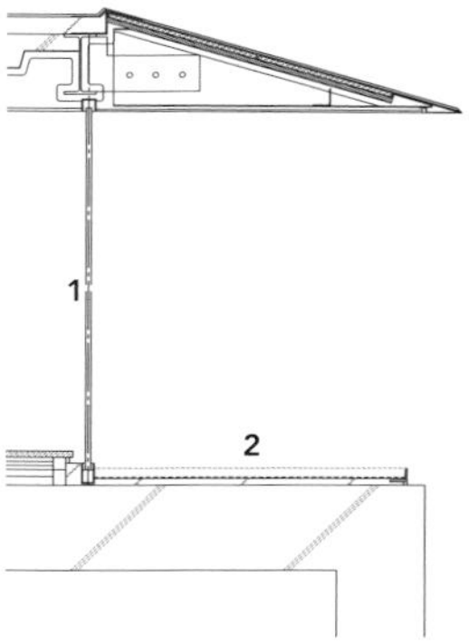

Detail, section through the terrace, sheltered by the roof overhang
1 bay window
2 water

On the terrace, the plane of water visually extends the surface of the ocean. The outdoor columns are made of galvanized steel. The detail on the carefully handled windows and the delicacy of the joinery emphasize visual continuity.

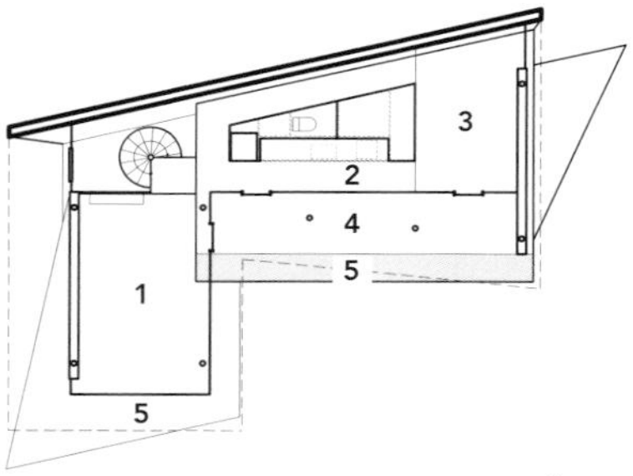

Upper-floor plan
1 living/dining area
2 kitchen
3 master bedroom
4 terrace
5 water

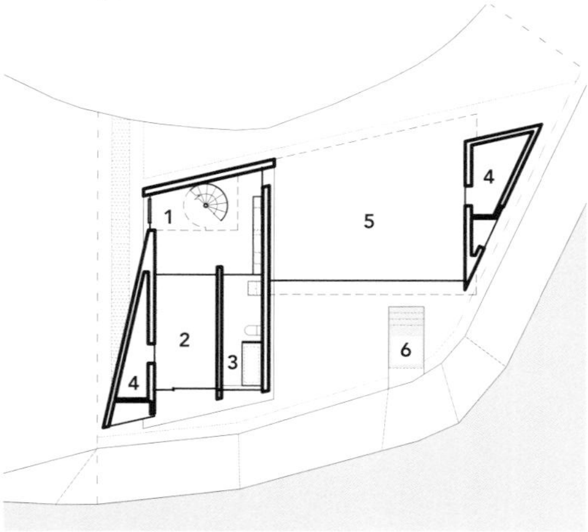

Ground-floor plan
1 entrance
2 guest bedroom
3 bathroom
4 storage
5 garage
6 swimming pool

Affordable House in Tewantin, Australia

Lacoste + Stevenson Architects

In Australia, the ability of architects to add to the landscape light and eco-friendly houses, well suited to the climate and relying on wood and metal, has already been proven. This house, designed by Lacoste + Stevenson, is set at the mouth of the Noosa River, on the Pacific Ocean. When the architects were approached, a small house from the 1930s already occupied the site. It was a modest residence, in wood, on pilotis. Typical of structures found in the state of Queensland, it opened to the channel on one side and to a national park on the other. The interior was only three cubic rooms, and the floor, walls, and ceilings were entirely covered in wood. Preserved in that state, they now house two bedrooms and the new kitchen.

The clients wanted a larger and more comfortable vacation house, where they could accommodate houseguests, and so the architects added two projecting wings. The first, facing the shore, houses a living/dining area that opens like a veranda. With its large sliding-glass doors and removable insect screens, this large longitudinal room can be reconfigured.

The second wing, oriented toward the national park, houses a bedroom, bathroom, WC, and a multipurpose space. All these rooms open onto a terrace via three large French windows that slide freely to offer many different relationships with the outdoors, depending on the time and season. The different materials underscore this variety: the first bay is in clear glass, the second in sandblasted glass, the third amounts to a simple insect screen. This system of light protection, which is very useful in summer for a house where the inside and the outside meld into one another, is equally valuable in winter, when the house is not occupied, for it prevents birds and other local creatures from nesting inside.

The wings, which double the size of the existing structure, consist of two timber portal frames running lengthwise. Thus freed from any structural requirements over 12 meters, the façades can open completely. The screen walls that extend the rhythm of the wooden weatherboards from the original house also make it possible to open the side façades to adapt to the tropical climate of this region and to provide natural ventilation for the house. The large overhang of the roof offers protection from the rain.

On the interior as on the exterior, the original structure can be easily made out, and the brightness of the addition contrasts with the darker ambience of the original house. This contrast recurs on the ceilings: the high timber ceilings of the main rooms differ from those in the extension, which are low and white and which frame the opening onto the water. The rainwater, which is collected on the roof, is stored under the house in four tanks with a total capacity of 20,000 liters.

The house under construction with, in the center, the small building originally on the site. The wooden portal frames give bulk to the two main façades in order to accommodate the two wings that constitute the addition.

Location: Tewantin, Queensland, Australia — Program: renovation and addition of a one-story vacation house with the creation of a new living room, dining room, kitchen, bedroom, bathroom, linen closet, and terrace — Owners: Peter and Lynnette Brown — Architect: Lacoste + Stevenson Architects — Surface area: interior space, 107 m² net living space; terrace, 24 m² — Cost of work: 164,000 euros — Schedule: 2002-04 — Building system and materials: structure entirely of wood, columns and truss beam system in wood with plywood facing, purlins, and rafters, flooring and louvred shutters in wood, French windows in aluminum, roof in corrugated iron. — General contractor: Ron Scholtes.

The rear façade, extended by a large terrace on pilotis, is oriented toward the national park.

On the north façade, one can clearly see where the original house ends and the addition begins.

Detail of the termite trap.

Section through the ocean façade, detail of the windows. The frame of the French windows disappears below floor level and above ceiling level.

1 steel spandrel beam
2 lining
3 plywood (9 mm)
4 mounting bracket
5 wood beam (150 x 50 cm)
6 aluminum sliding door
7 wood ceiling (19 mm)
8 hollow pointing
9 hollow pointing in silicone
10 wood floor (19 mm)
11 aluminum sliding door
12 mounting bracket
13 wood beam (150 x 50 cm)
14 steel structural beam

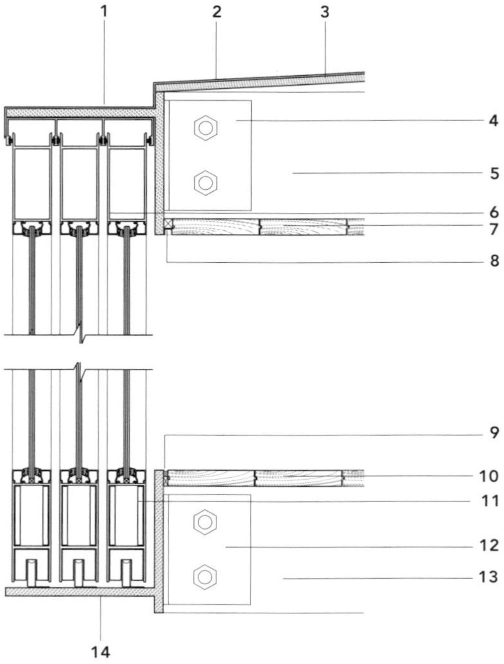

The addition, oriented toward the sea, houses the living room and the dining room in a large veranda.

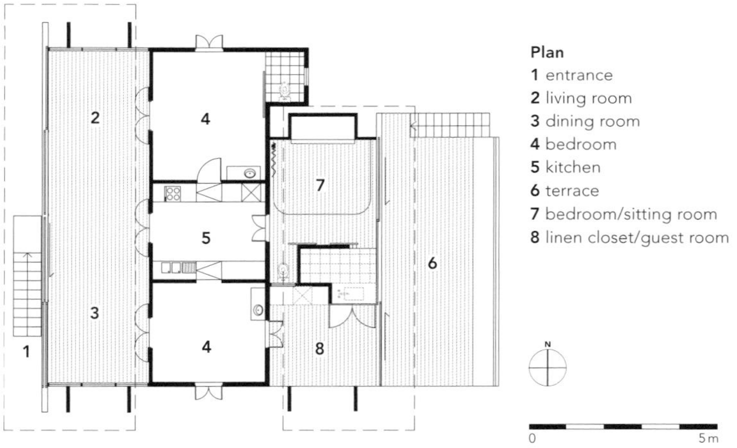

Plan
1 entrance
2 living room
3 dining room
4 bedroom
5 kitchen
6 terrace
7 bedroom/sitting room
8 linen closet/guest room

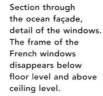

A FEW WORDS FROM THE ARCHITECT

"In this house, the overhang of the roof is substantial, for it protects the house from the strong tropical rains. The roof shelters the structure of the house, hardwood columns and beams made of pine sandwiched between two sheets of plywood. The plywood is varnished, as on a boat, and should be re-varnished every two or three years. The top of the wood columns carries a metal lining that makes it possible to protect the house from termites (termites do not like the light). The rest of the house has painted wood siding that must be repainted every ten years; aluminum joinery needs no upkeep, and glass, lots of glass..."

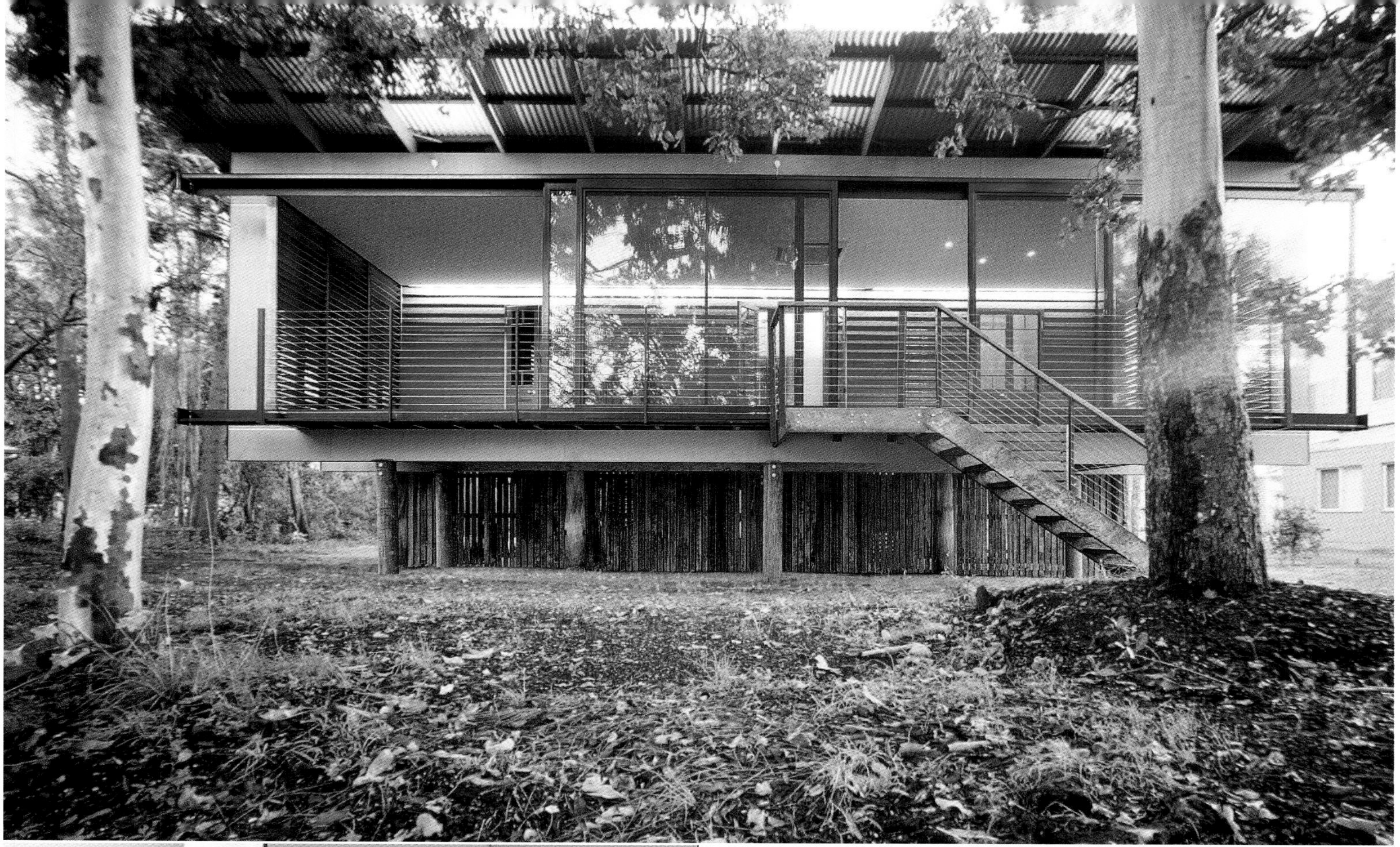

Village House in Corrubedo, Spain

David Chipperfield Architects

Reveling in tradition and context, drawing inspiration from familiar structures to create a contemporary architecture on a given site, such are the gymnastics that the British architect David Chipperfield likes to employ. In this spirit and with the restraint that is part of his vocabulary, he built a vacation house on the Atlantic coast, in a Galacian village near the Portuguese border, exploring the typology of a town house at the water's edge. At the far end of a very protected bay, the site features a splendid view of the port and the sea.
While seeking a delicate complicity with the vernacular setting, with its humble materials and play of shadows, the architect also liberates himself from it: "Our house is in the heart of a fishing village; I noticed that, very curiously, the local houses have no large windows and that they turn their backs to the sea, facing instead the enclosed spaces of the village – perhaps because the water brings worry? Thus we entered into this context while also setting ourselves apart from it. As the house was to be inserted between two existing houses, we picked up their geometries and their small windows, but we added a 'bridge space' that fits in with the roofline and blends with the surroundings. In this way, we took advantage of a space oriented toward the sea, which the other residents do not possess." Seen from the sea, the silhouette of the village is a massive residential band, unified despite the disparity in height and shape. The new house is wedged into this residential wall, finding a more contemporary expression through its volumes that combine porosity, framing, and recessing. Facing the sea, a stone and concrete base with small windows identical to those of the neighboring houses ensures continuity. The first floor features an enormous panoramic window, extending the entire width of the house. Above, the volume shifts and becomes more complex: framing, extra thickness, and deeper-set openings give the house its identity. Formal appropriation becomes apparent on the façade oriented toward the town, where the contrasting geometry of the neighboring houses dictates the composition.
On the interior, this concept extends to the stairs, the bedrooms, and the living spaces, which flow freely up to the top of the house, mixing outdoors and indoors according to an organic logic. On the second floor, a small loggia overlooking the beach leads to the bedrooms, and from there to the roof terrace. With its angles and white walls, this house by the vacationing English architect is introduced with respect, yet it reenergizes the picture-postcard image of this village.

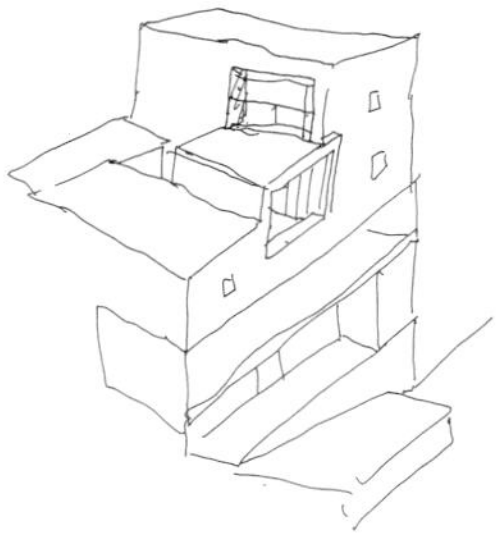

Location: Corrubedo, Galicia, Spain — Program: seafront vacation house with three stories, comprising six bedrooms, a large living room, loggia, and terrace — Owner: David Chipperfield — Architect: David Chipperfield Architects; David Chipperfield, project manager; Louise Brooker, Luca Donadoni, Pablo Gallego Picard, Ricardo Iboim Ingles, Victoria Jessen-Pike, Daniel Lopez-Perez, Carlos Martínez de Albornoz, Tina Sophie Müller, Anat Talmor, Oliver Ulmer, Giuseppe Zampieri, architects; Carlos Fontenla and Carlos Seoane, associate architects — Technical consultants for structure: Jane Wernick Associates; Jane Wernick, Javier Estevez Cimadevila — Surface area: 210 m² net living space — Cost of work: not disclosed — Schedule: 1996-2002 — General contractor: Serinfra SA.

In alignment with the other buildings in the port, the house fills an empty space. Unlike its neighbors, it opens up to the ocean.

ALARMA

In the living room, spartan furniture obscures everything, save the panoramic bay and the landscape.

Between the rocks on the beach, the stone base, and the ceramic facing on the neighboring house, the lines and the materials take shape gradually. The floor of the second level aligns with the horizon. Above, the house finds its own logic.

Bottom left:
On the second floor, the living room, sparely furnished so as to feature the ocean view.

Bottom right:
The entrance façade, facing the village.

The terrace is protected from the wind by a thick railing that also serves as a bench.

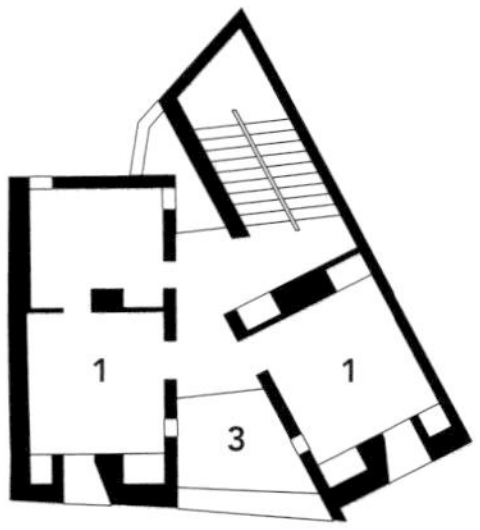

Second-floor plan.

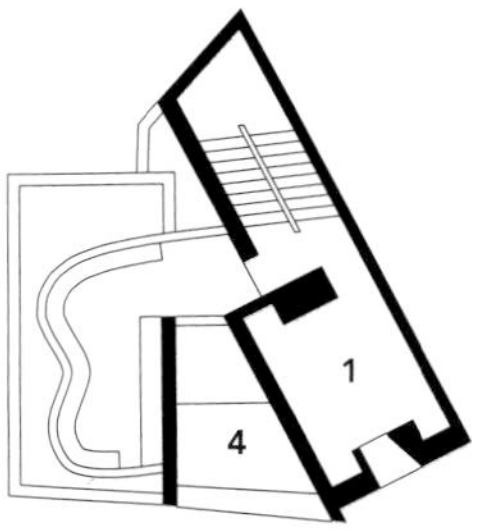

Third-floor plan.

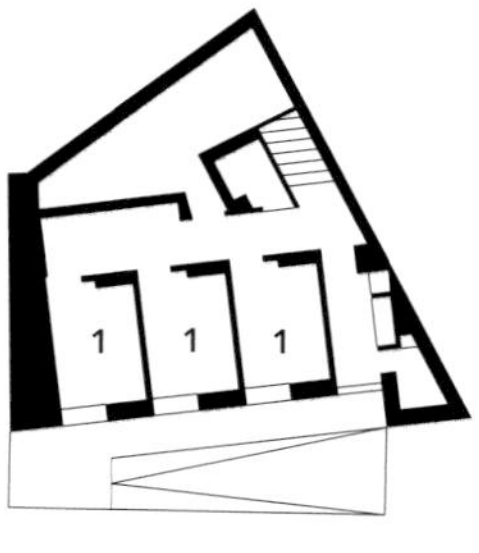

Ground-floor plan.

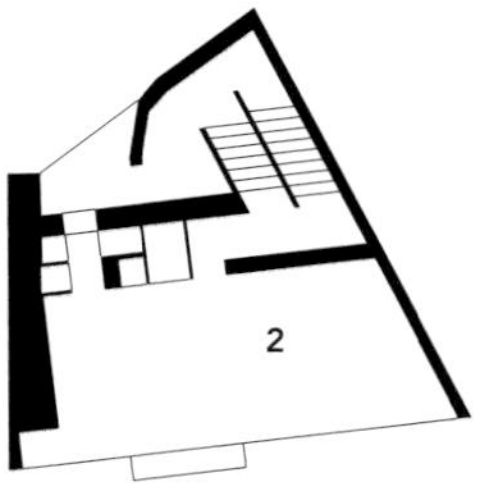

First-floor plan.

1 bedroom
2 living room
3 loggia
4 terrace

0 5m

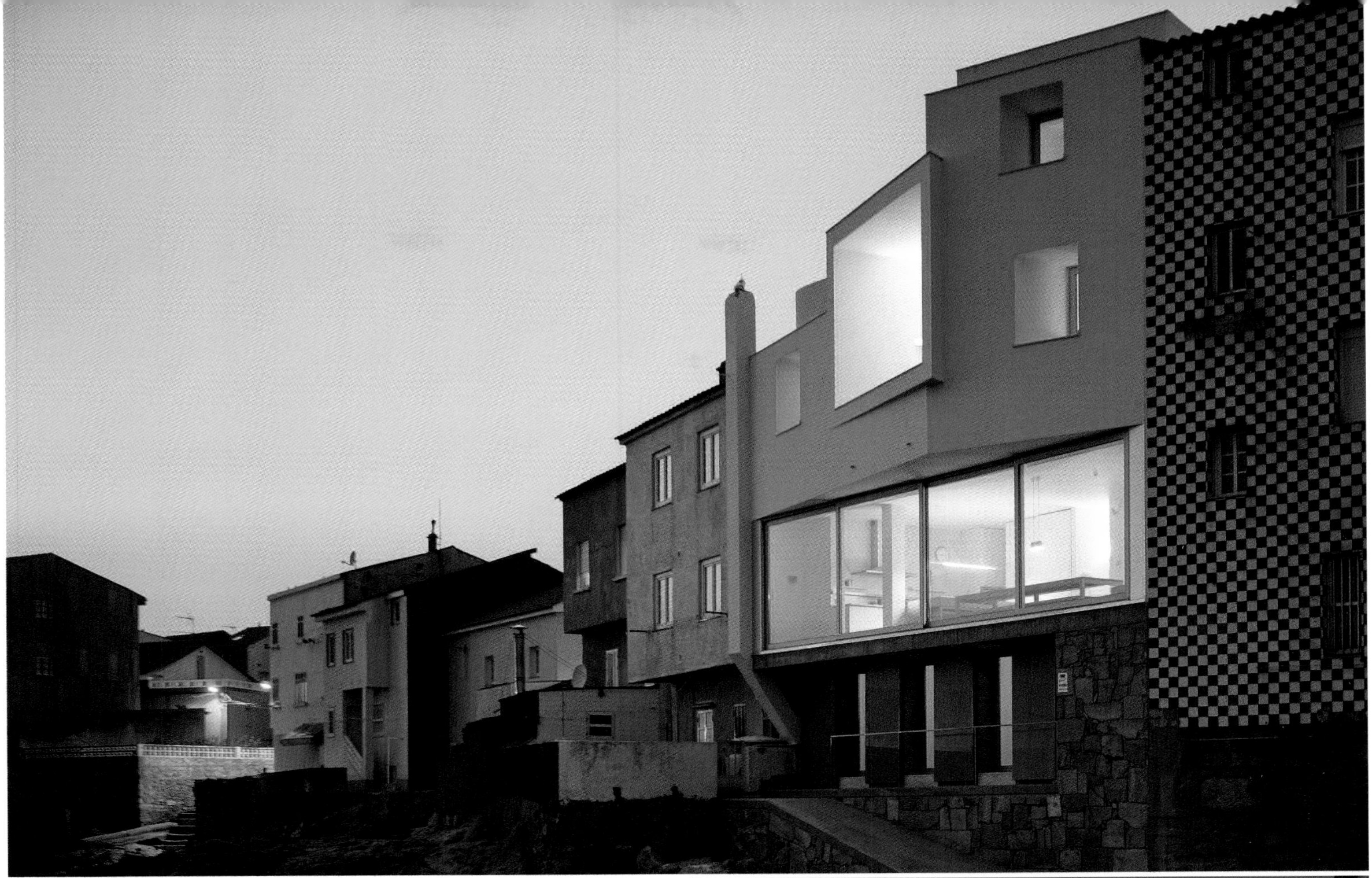

Polymer House in Dungeness, Great Britain

Simon Conder

After row upon row of traditional Victorian structures in coastal villages, England saw the blossoming, in the 1930s, of more helter-skelter settlements along the beaches. In order to remedy the situation, the town of Dungeness, not far from Dover, created a protected site where all construction was prohibited. It is in this context that the architect Simon Conder renovated and expanded a dilapidated fisherman's cottage. Built over time, it was itself the product of successive, more or less random additions; it is surprising that the cottage resisted the force of the wind for so long.

The limited budget of the client compelled the architect to opt for inexpensive materials, which explains the innovative use of a black synthetic rubber of the polymer EPDM (Ethylene Propylene Diene Monomer) variety. EPDM is an industrial product generally used for waterproofing terraces. Thus an unexpected domestic architecture unfolded, which adds an unusual touch to the improbable setting, having as a backdrop the silhouette of a power station.

When the dismantling of the roof and original walls revealed a very rotten frame, what began as a simple renovation ended up as a structure that was three-quarters new. The existing structure was expanded to the south and east to capture the views. The new wood structure is windbraced by large plywood panels, which eliminate the internal finishes. This material is also used for the walls, parquet floors, ceilings, doors, and joinery.

On the exterior, the synthetic rubber, cut to size in the factory, covers all the walls and the roof. Each component was cut in a large sheet of EPDM, including the joints, with the assembly and connections handled on-site. The envelope is waterproof, and the rainwater drainage system does not require the addition of unsightly gutters.

As the priority was to optimize the surface area of the living spaces, the interior has only one small bedroom. It adjoins the bathroom, where the raised bathtub features a view of the sea. When houseguests come, they stay in a 1950s Airstream trailer parked next to the house, where its aluminum exterior contrasts with the black volume.

On this beach on the English Channel, the houses face difficult climate conditions and must withstand strong winds. According to the architect, the industrial standards for EPDM polymer meet these requirements. This waterproof material is also resistant to ozone, UV rays, haze, and temperatures from -50 to +130 degrees. What is more, it is malleable and durable.

The original shed, transformed into an entryway.

Location: Dungeness, Great Britain — Program: reorganization and expansion of a small fisherman's hut, with a kitchen/dining area, sitting room, living area, bedroom, and bathroom — Owner: private — Architect: Simon Conder — Surface area: 90 m^2 net living space — Cost of work: not disclosed — Schedule: completion, November 2003 — Building system and materials: wood structure, waterproof EPDM envelope — Contractors: Charlier Construction and AAC Waterproofing.

The house, complemented by a trailer for house guests, gives the setting the air of a road movie.

At the far end of the sitting room, the terrace is oriented toward the coast.

The bathroom opens toward the beach.

Plan
1 deck
2 kitchen/dining area
3 living room
4 living space
5 wood stove
6 storage
7 bedroom
8 bathroom
9 raised bathtub
10 glazed lobby
11 entrance
12 street
13 trailer

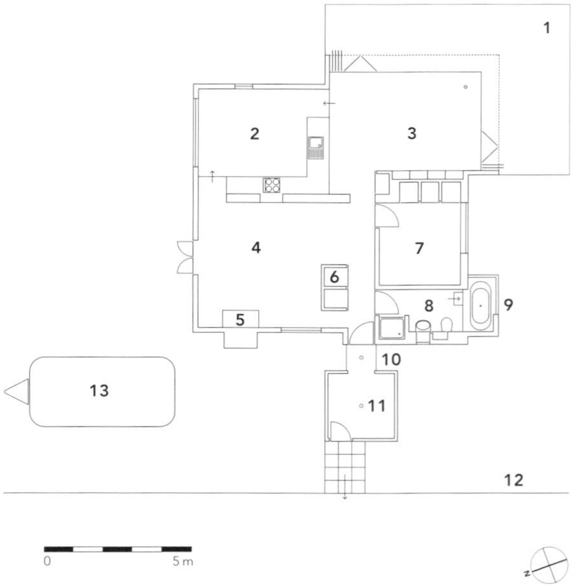

A FEW WORDS FROM THE ARCHITECT

"The plywood that covers the wood frame comes from Finnish forests managed in accordance with ecological principles. Because the distinctive feature of the coastal setting is the wind, rubber facing seemed to be a good environmental solution. In summer, the windows remain open so as to create a flow of air that makes up for the heat generated by the material. In winter, when the windows are closed, the synthetic black rubber retains warmth, making it possible to reduce the heating.

The southern façade with the extension features sliding bay windows; the raised bathtub nestles in the volume projecting from the façade.

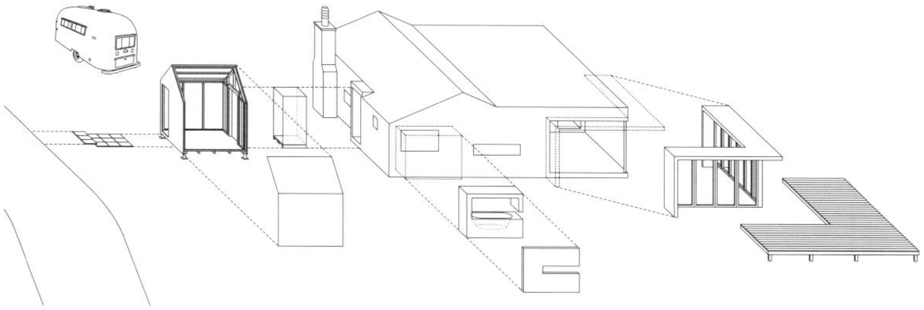

Photogenic contrasts between the black rubber and the polished aluminum of the Airstream trailer.

The extension, living-room side; in the background is the Dungeness power station.

Insular House near Stockholm, Sweden

Claesson Koivisto Rune Arkitektkontor

In the Stockholm archipelago, on a coastal point only 4 meters from the shores of the Baltic Sea, this little summer house creates its own Robinson Crusoe myth. It is a residence for a young couple with three children; they just finished work on a large family house set on a hill 8 meters away. The surface area allowed by planning regulations reduced the livable space to 45 square meters. "Whether the surface area of a project is 45 or 4,500 square meters, the work is the same! This house, which required many sketches and detail drawings, is without doubt one of the most successful projects that we have done," its designers assert. "For us, it is a good illustration of the well-known adage 'Small is beautiful.' We belong to the same family as the client, and we have known each other for a long time; this additional constraint meant that we could not make any mistakes!"
To detach from the visual proximity and protect everyone's privacy, the façade facing the main house is totally blank. On the opposite side, facing the sea, the house opens wide to take in the views. It follows the topography of the site, which dictated its shape and volume: its plan avoids a ravine, accentuating a slight fold. This inspired the architects to design a hybrid roof that, despite the small scale, make it possible for them to introduce variety in the interior spaces. The tallest spaces (2.8 to 3.4 meters) are for the living room and kitchen; these two rooms are covered with a simple pent roof, whose ridge piece extends diagonally to the lower wing (2.3 to 2.8 meters), which houses the bedrooms. On this rocky site, among the coastal pines, a close relationship is forged between the site, the plan of the house, and its curious roof.
To reconcile the restrictions of the ground with the requirements of a program calling for two bedrooms, an entryway, a kitchen/living room, and storage space proved difficult; but, because of a visual extension into the landscape, none of the rooms feels cramped. All the windows, whether vertical (as in the bedrooms) or more square (in the living areas), were designed and worked with care, giving the residents the feeling of lift up to the roof line. The beveled upper parts of the window leaves blend with the façades, creating the illusion of a very thin roof.
The pine façades are protected with an application of iron vitriol, giving the house a gray tint in the sunlight. This is a popular technique in Sweden when building in a coastal region. Insulation is ensured by double glazing, and heat comes from a wood stove.

Location: Kråkmora Holmar Island, Stockholm archipelago, Sweden — Program: vacation house for a couple with three children comprising an entryway, living room, kitchen, and two bedrooms — Owners: Fredrik and Sanna Claesson — Architect: Claesson Koivisto Rune Arkitektkontor AB; Mårten Claesson, Eero Koivisto, Ola Rune, Deta Gemzell, architects — Surface area: 45 m^2 net living space — Cost of work: not disclosed — Schedule: 2003-05 — Building system and materials: wood construction on concrete slab — General contractor: Larsson & Co AB.

To build this house so close to the sea, all the materials were brought in by boat, as the construction site was difficult to access.

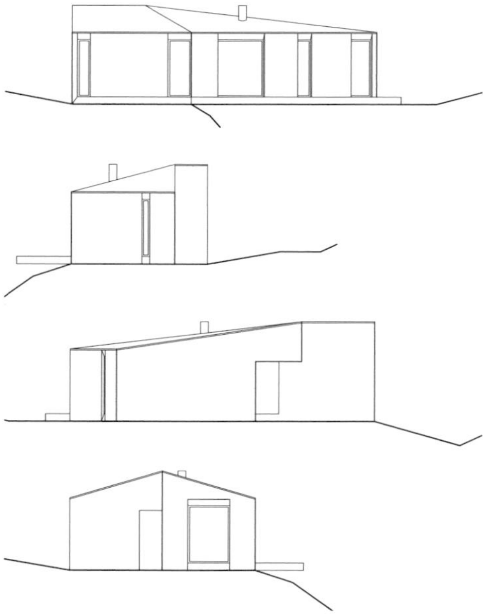

From top to bottom: the east, north, west, and south façades.

The colors of the house blend with those of the countryside. The windows are like an echo of the glinting water.

On a rocky site among the maritime pines, this structure with spare volumes slips away before the Baltic Sea.

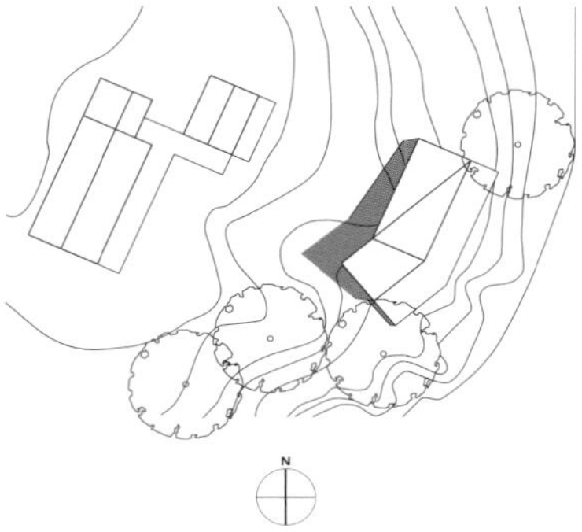

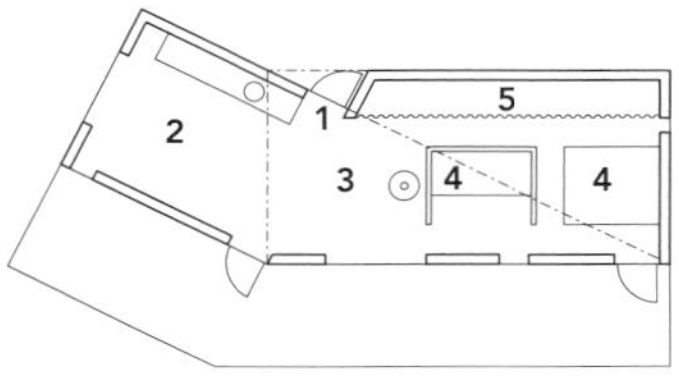

Plan
1 entrance
2 kitchen
3 living room
4 bedroom
5 closets

0 5 m

At the foot of the hill, the entrance offers a transverse view to the sea.

Beach House in Las Arenas, Peru

Javier Artadi

With the aim of exploring the possibilities of a beach house and its adaptation to a variety of uses, architect Javier Artadi built this 215-square-meter house on Las Arenas beach, 100 kilometers south of Lima. Unlike the uneven terrain of La Escondida beach (see page 132), this one stretches out flat toward the water. For years, the housing developments running along the coast have gained ground on the desert landscape, gradually forming actual urban islets on the beaches. Here, according to the current specifications, each parcel can have two houses, which makes it necessary to protect the privacy of each one. The house is allied with a box in which a large trapezoidal container holds the living room, dining room, terrace, and swimming pool. On the interior of this volume, a whole line of furniture designed by the architect was incorporated (sofa, storage unit, chaises longues, and so on).

To frame strategic views while also controlling the light, the design of the façades and roof develop a contrast between opacity and a skillful arrangement of slots and openings. The west façade opens onto the swimming pool and terrace. Raised up a step from the ground, the latter gives the residents a feeling of freedom that fits well with the spirit of seaside houses. Thus it seems to levitate above the lawn of an unexpected garden; as the architect explains, "in a climate where it is necessary to protect oneself from the dust of the desert, the garden becomes an essential component." Surrounding the main volume, the bedrooms and the secondary spaces stretch out behind the north and east façades, spaced along an oblique axis that meets up with the pool. An open-air entryway separates the living room from the master bedroom. These two rooms are lit by two large bay windows that visually link the bedroom to the terrace and, by extension, to the horizon. By raising the terrace, the architect freed up the basement space for a television-viewing area, tucked into a niche in the incline of the site. It is lit naturally by an opalescent glass cupola located near the entrance. Perpendicular to the sea and adjoining the neighboring propriety, the north façade is totally blank. Free and independent in its mass, the box thus asserts its autonomy, and the space occupied by the swimming pool provides it with a protective screen. Playful and functional, this residence identifies the traditional uses of a beach house. The constant mildness of the climate is favorable to its formal freedom and to natural ventilation throughout the year. Its concrete structure and brick walls covered with plastered stucco were executed by local craftsmen. The stucco and aluminum joinery of the doors and windows are sufficient protection from the seaside atmosphere.

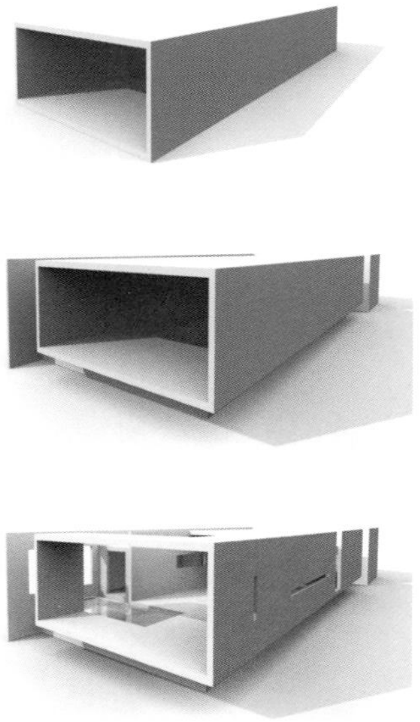

Illustration of a real-estate policy: a site in transformation, where developments are slowly gaining on the beach.

Location: Las Arenas beach, Lima, Peru — Program: two-story beach house with terrace and swimming pool, comprising a living room, dining room, four bedrooms, five bathrooms, a kitchen, laundry area, television room — Owner: private — Architect: Javier Artadi — Technical consultants: for structure, Jorge Indacochea; for electricity, Rigoberto Mayorga; for plumbing, Angel dall'Orto — Surface area: 215 m^2 net living space — Cost of work: 54,850 euros, or approximately 260 euros per m^2 — Schedule: completion, January 2004 — Building system and materials: concrete structure, brick and stucco walls — General contractor: Justo Olivera.

Four steps to life on a platform raised off the ground, where interior and exterior flow together.

The television room in the basement, lit from above.

The southern façade. When night falls, the lighting showcases the house, as if it were suspended over the lawn.

Open to the sky but protected from the wind, the terrace is an integral room where the furniture designed by the architect contributes to the overall composition.

The swimming pool runs beside the kitchen, where a ribbon window also serves as a serving hatch.

The rear façade, closed to protect the privacy of the residents.

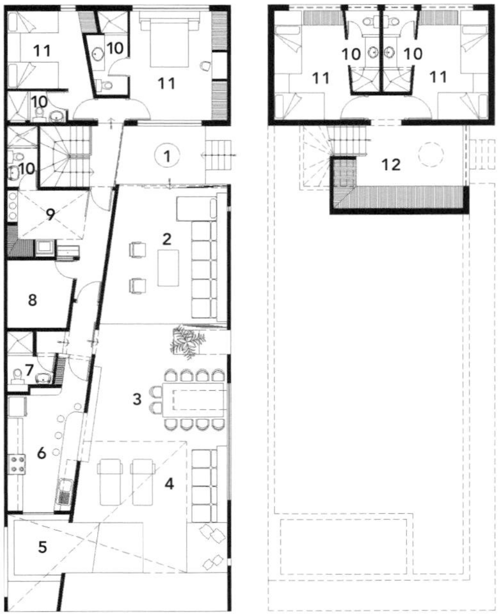

Ground-floor and basement plans
1 entrance
2 living room
3 dining room
4 terrace
5 swimming pool
6 kitchen
7 WC
8 storage
9 laundry area
10 bathroom
11 bedroom
12 television room

0 5m

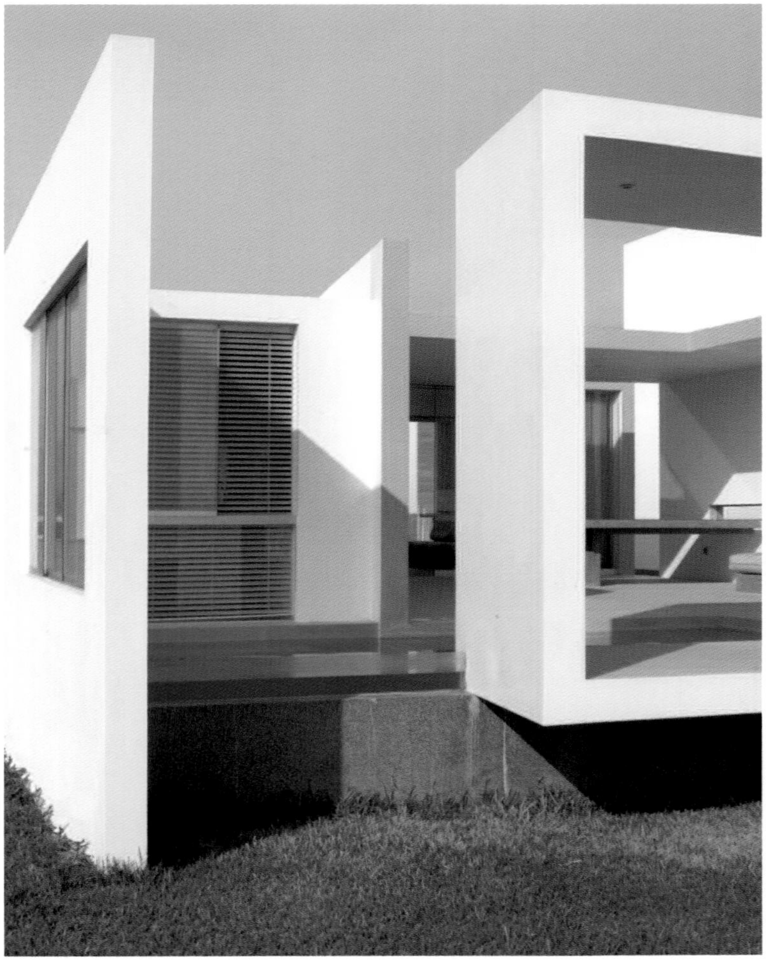

Strategic openings along the façade frame the views and control the light.

3 The House Tucked Away on the Site

Sheltered Villa in Hovås, Sweden

Wingårdh Arkitektkontor

With a design "inspired by the drama of the Swedish coast," the Villa Astrid is very well suited to its site: a rocky parcel adjoining a pine forest, on a cliff that is accessible by a path. For the architect, Gerth Wingårdh, this house on a particularly uneven site is, from the technical standpoint, the most interesting that he has ever built. The complexity of the site and the oblique angle of the cliff with regard to the view were the challenges that, coupled with the planning regulations requiring the slope of roofs to be between 14 and 30 degrees, had a direct influence on the architectural concept.
The house is one with the rock, which affects the interiors, stands out on the exterior, and forms one of the walls of the courtyard that brings light to the lower-level rooms. These rooms, at entry level, take full advantage of the ocean views thanks to the way the building twists around: all the glazed openings, punched in the prepatinated copper that covers the façades and the roof like a shield, yet without obscuring the transparency, were carefully designed. In this way, a permanent relationship is set up between the sea, nature, and the interior spaces. Under the copper shell, the totally impermeable structure is made of reinforced-concrete beams resting on walls of aerated concrete insulated by glass wool.
In reality, the house is deceptive in the play on the volumes. If, at the entry, it appears to be a relatively low, light-filled house, the courtyard atrium, in direct contact with the rocks, creates a surprise by revealing a sudden verticality. "What seemed to be a low building changes into a three-story structure. To reinforce this effect, giving the illusion of a six-story building, I even thought of covering the floor of the courtyard with a water mirror. But as practical concerns took priority, I had to abandon the idea, especially as this courtyard provides the family with a warm outdoor shelter, comfortable and protected from the ocean breezes, where the children can play," explains the architect.
An enormous open kitchen, dining room, and living area divide the entry floor. At the far end, a mezzanine overlooks a cascade of rocks. On the lower level, the three bedrooms each enjoy a direct opening to the outdoors.
The side wall facing the rock joins with an immense insulated-glass window that fits into a cleft carved in the rock. Shortly after its construction, a Japanese garden was added to the house. Near the rear entrance door and the kitchen, it provides a select spot for observation.

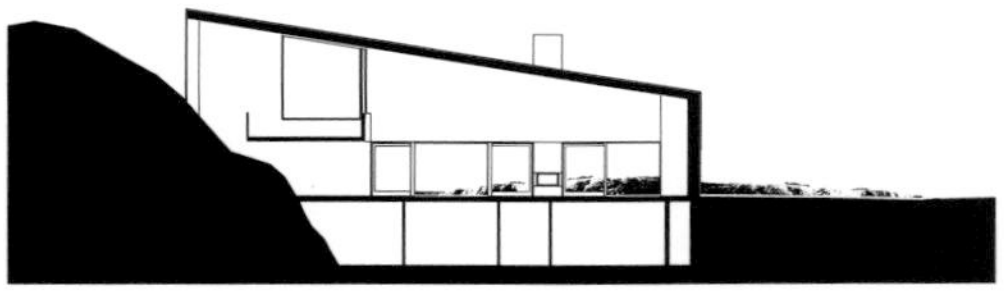

Location: Hovås, municipality of Gothenburg, Sweden — Program: family house with two stories and a mezzanine, comprising a living room, kitchen, dining room, three bedrooms, two bathrooms, and a laundry room — Owner: private — Architect: Wingårdh Arkitektkontor AB; Gert Wingårdh and Karin Wingårdh, project managers; Joakim Lyth, assistant — Technical consultant for structure: Danuta Nielsen — Surface area: 400 m² net living space — Cost of work: 1.1 million euros — Schedule: construction, 2003-04 — Building system and materials: poured-in-place concrete, aerated concrete, façade and roof in prepatinated copper, Outokumpu — Contractors: general contractor, FB Engineering AB; plumbing, NVK VVS Kontroll AB; electricity, Schönbeck Elprojekt AB.

A prepatinated copper shield, for protection from coastal winds, surrounds the large glazed rooms facing the sea. The color of the copper echoes that of the water.

The glass that covers the side wall fits into a slot cut in the rock.

The roof consists of a poured-in-place concrete structure, insulated with glass wool and covered with metal. Because of the climate and in order to avoid corrosion, the envelope has no openings. The chimney is outdoors, and the ducts run in the walls.

On one side, the sea; on the other, the rock of the cliff, omnipresent.

Detail of section through the façade of the interior courtyard

1 copper mounting bracket (0.7 mm)
2 waterproofing in porous glass wool (150 mm) attached with metal brackets
3 structural concrete (150 x 356 mm)
4 plaster rendering (10 mm)
5 concrete (400 mm)
6 copper sheet (0.7 mm) on a thickness of approximately 415 mm
7 parquet (8 mm)
8 coating (17 mm) and concrete (160 mm)
9 porous glass wool (50 mm)
10 glazed sliding door (2,135 mm)
11 sliding door (2,510 mm)

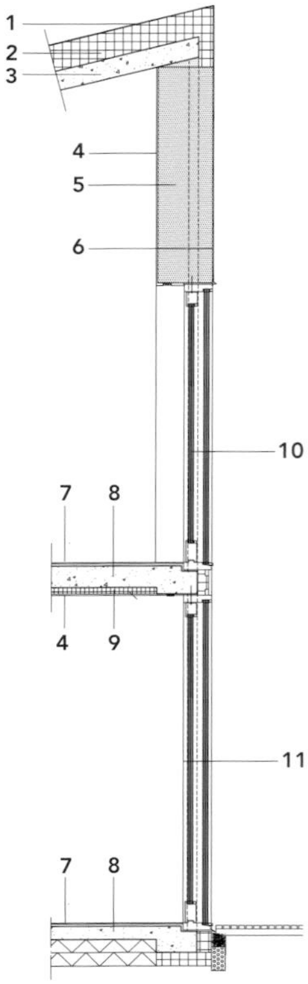

The use of simple materials was favored. The aerated concrete walls are rendered, then clad on the exterior with prepatinated copper whose color turns verdigris. To avoid corrosion of the floor and the problems of upkeep, the copper ions are neutralized by the addition of crushed limestone around the foundations.

Modern conveniences and a carefully planned set-up for a house that is confronted with variations in the climate and the landscape.

The courtyard, a shelter left open to the sky, serves as a lightwell for the bedrooms, located on the lower level.

Warmed by the floors and the wood furniture, the dining room and living room are large free spaces opening to the outdoors. At the far end of the living room, the mezzanine.

The rock is incorporated into the bathroom.

1 bedroom
2 bathroom
3 laundry room
4 kitchen
5 dining area
6 living room
7 mezzanine
8 terrace
9 interior courtyard

0 5 10 m

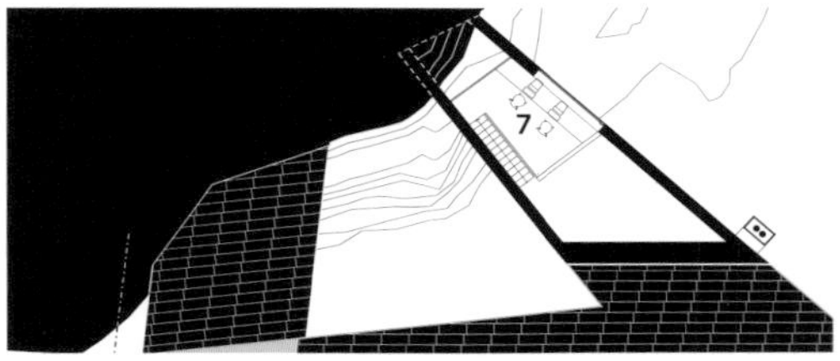

Plan of the mezzanine.

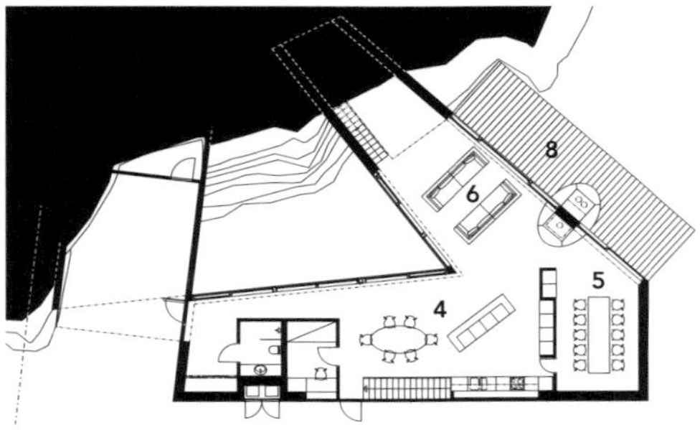

Plan of the entrance level.

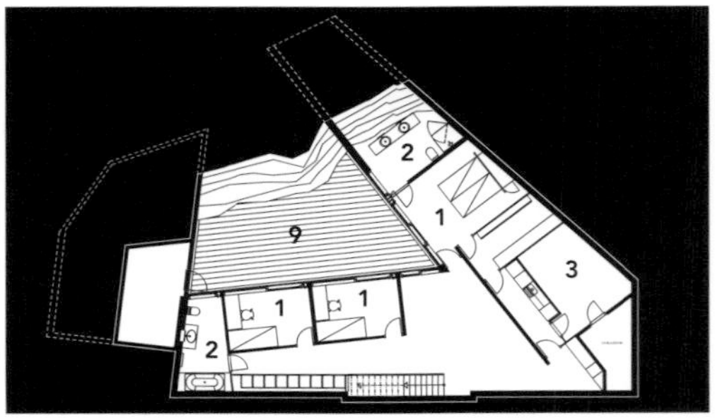

Plan of the lower level.

A frosted glass screen separates the staircase. On the lower level, the bedrooms open onto the courtyard via large sliding doors.

Chameleon House in La Escondida, Peru

Sandra Barclay and Jean-Pierre Crousse

With its glazed swimming pool that pretends to be mistaken for a giant aquarium perched high above the sea, this house is one of a group of vacation houses located in a seismic area on La Escondida beach in Peru. In this part of the world, temperatures hardly vary throughout the year, but it is important to protect oneself from the sun's rays, which come down vertically.

The house occupies all of the buildable volume of the parcel. "During the design phase of the project, this virtual volume (11 meters by 25 meters by 3.6 meters high) was dug to create living spaces, a bit like archaeologists who dig by removing sand to reveal pre-Columbian ruins. This mentality of design by subtraction, which goes against the mentality of addition in the act of building, is applied at all the scales of the project to make it intelligible, and the various spaces are modified by their distinct relationships with the sky and the sea," explain the architects. The house becomes a falsely introverted enclosure in search of openness toward the sea, the sand, and the horizon.

It is also a device for framing that thwarts the mono-orientation of the parcel by multiplying the points of view. Indoor and outdoor spaces, with or without roofing, overlap, making one forget the relative narrowness of the original plot. Depending on the rooms and the functions, the proportions alternately favor privacy and hospitality, and the living spaces provide beautiful views.

From the entrance, the patio extends toward the ocean via a large terrace, a horizontal plane visually connected to the horizon by the long, narrow swimming pool.

A portico crosses the width of the enclosure and frames the ocean setting while also acting like a large parasol to shelter the living and dining areas. Sliding glass panels blur the boundaries between the living room and the terrace. Following the slope of the site, a gently rising staircase leads to the sleeping area set under the terrace, which protects the rooms from the sun. The intermediary level extends laterally, leading to the guest room and children's rooms. A loggia, set below the staircase and under the swimming pool, leads to the parents' bedroom.

Having designed this house at their firm in Paris, the architects wanted to rationalize the structure and simplify the details in order to facilitate the work of the local laborers. The frame, of poured-in-place reinforced concrete, is completed by a traditional masonry filling. By picking up ochre shades, present in pre-Columbian and colonial structures on the Peruvian coast, the architects ensure that the accumulation of dust and desert sand will not age the walls prematurely. Applied on the entire exterior of the house, the sand color also shows unity with the outer wall. All superfluous details are eliminated, and the architecture retains the strength of its structure in the face of the absolute order of the ocean setting.

Location: La Escondida beach, Cañete province, Peru — Program: vacation house with a swimming pool and terraces, comprising a living/dining area, kitchen, and four bedrooms — Owner: private — Architects: Sandra Barclay and Jean-Pierre Crousse; Edward Barclay, architectural oversight — Surface area: site, 253 m^2; building, 174 m^2 total floor area — Cost of work: 65,000 euros — Schedule: design, June – September 2002; construction, October 2002 – February 2003; completion, March 2003 — Building system and materials: concrete curtains, foundation curtains for the areas with the heaviest loads, and reinforced beams approximately 80 cm deep running between them; partitions and soffits in untreated concrete, floors and architectural furnishings in waxed concrete; deck, floor, partitions, doors and furniture in Diable Fuerte (an Amazonian wood); tempered glass for the stationary and sliding doors without frames; cement rendering and paint for the exterior and interior walls — General contractor: Constructora Edward Barclay.

A key component of the house, the swimming pool also plays an essential role in framing views.

The living/dining area, protected from the wind and opening onto the terrace.

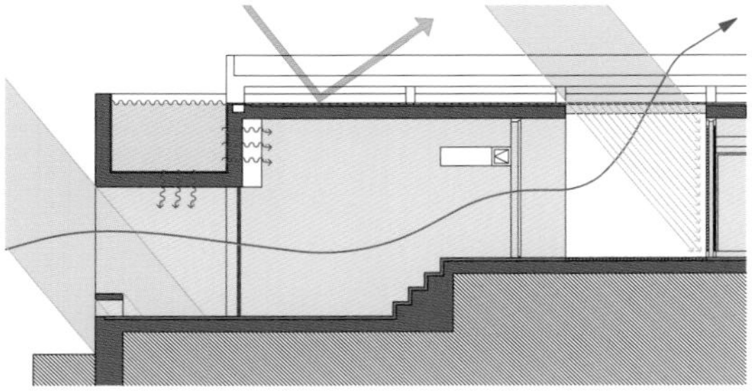

Detail of the section and brise-soleil.

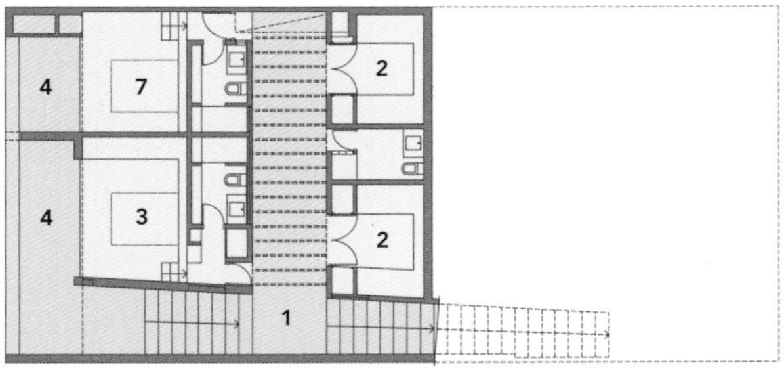

Lower-level plan.

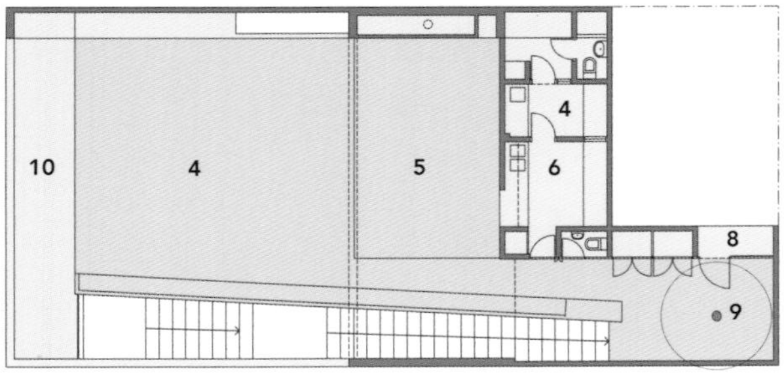

Upper-level plan.

1 entrance, beach side
2 children's room
3 parents' bedroom
4 terrace
5 living/dining room
6 kitchen
7 guest room
8 entrance, street side
9 patio
10 swimming pool

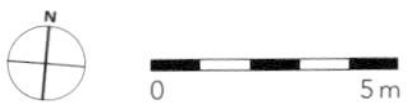

A FEW WORDS CONCERNING THE SWIMMING POOL:
The pool, set inside the surrounding walls, is made of cast concrete; the floors and the bench, which also serves as a railing for the terrace, are in concrete, which local artisans polished by hand. The pool slab is 25 centimeters thick. It has old wood formwork whose imprint is preserved by the concrete. Owing to the proximity of the sea, the concrete was covered with a cement rendering before being painted. The bench was made with a plywood formwork, and the application of a cement coating floated by hand softens the corners.

The gently rising staircase that leads to the bedrooms opens a cleft in the house volume, leaving the pool "to float" on the ocean.

Opposite page:
The entrance on the street side, at the top of the dune; the almost blind walls protect the privacy of the house.

Borrowed from the pre-Columbian palette, the ochre and sand hues play on their mimetism with the desert ground. On the interior, these colors give way to white punctuated with touches of pink.

Cloister House in Victoria, Australia

Denton Corker Marshall

In a natural, protected setting two hours' drive from Melbourne, the grandiose context seems to be "at the end of the world." So is it a surprise that this cliff, battered by the wind, seduced the architect Barrie Marshall when he decided to build his weekend house? Faithful to the spare architectural vocabulary and contextual approach of Denton Corker Marshall, the owner/architect deliberately broke with the concepts of residence and domesticity in order to develop the idea of camouflage, in an agricultural area where large, scattered farms preside over properties of several hectares. Buried in the dunes, the house is hidden like a subversive bunker in which dark gray concrete draws substance from a black limestone promontory.
Seen from the opposite beach, the residence amounts to a long façade covered with tufts of grass; on the land side, it disappears, totally hidden in the site.
In designing this introverted house between the sea and the countryside, the architects expressed their desire not to compete with the natural setting, but rather showcase it. Out of this "retreat" came at last a strong aesthetic decision: the house makes one think of a protective bastion but also of a site for meditation.
The structure consists of a long, rectangular concrete box extended by a 3-meter-high wall that surrounds a large square courtyard. "Although the neighboring properties are rather far away, the surrounding countryside, with its large stretches of short grass, is not particularly pleasant," say the architects. "The courtyard therefore focuses attention on the sky and the ocean." On the ocean façade, the proportions and the location of each window were designed so as to frame views. A haven of peace in the immense landscape, the courtyard provides protection from the wind. In the middle of winter, it captures the sun. The concrete walls are built up against the dunes, whose slope covers the roof. Opposite the access route, a detached garage creates an opening in one of the walls.
On the interior, the rectangular plan makes it possible to align three bedrooms and two bathrooms, a kitchen/dining area, a wintergarden, living room, and laundry room. All the bedrooms, set along a single hall, can be closed off by doors that fold away to one side. When they are open, all the rooms have ocean views, and thus the hall becomes a flexible space that extends the living room.
In this region where the very harsh winters give way to hot summers, the issues of thermal comfort and insulation are resolved very simply by exterior walls without insulation, a simple treatment of windows, and electric floor heating. By absorbing the heat of the sun, the black concrete of the façade warms the interior of the house, which makes electric heat unnecessary except when it is very cold. As a general rule, the indoor temperature varies from 17 to 24 degrees Celsius (63 to 75 degrees Fahrenheit), and in summer, the ocean breezes cool the house during the night. Despite the proximity to the ocean, the concrete did not undergo any special treatment, but the fact that it was made from material found on site and poured in place proved relatively expensive, as the site is very isolated and the contractor had to do the work over six months.

Location: Phillip Island, Victoria, Australia — Program: weekend house with three bedrooms, two bathrooms, a wintergarden, living room, kitchen/dining area, and a garage for three cars — Owner: Barrie Marshall — Architect: Denton Corker Marshall — Technical consultant for structure: Arup — Surface area: 240 m² net living space — Cost of work: 300,000 euros — Schedule: completion, 1992 — Materials: dark gray concrete terrazzo flooring; outdoor spotlights, 30-60 cm in diameter; hot-dip galvanized steel windows; organic roof of natural grass — General contractor: Needham Construction.

The only part of the house visible from the beach below is a long façade punctuated by high vertical windows.

The roof, covered with short grass, emerges from the dune.

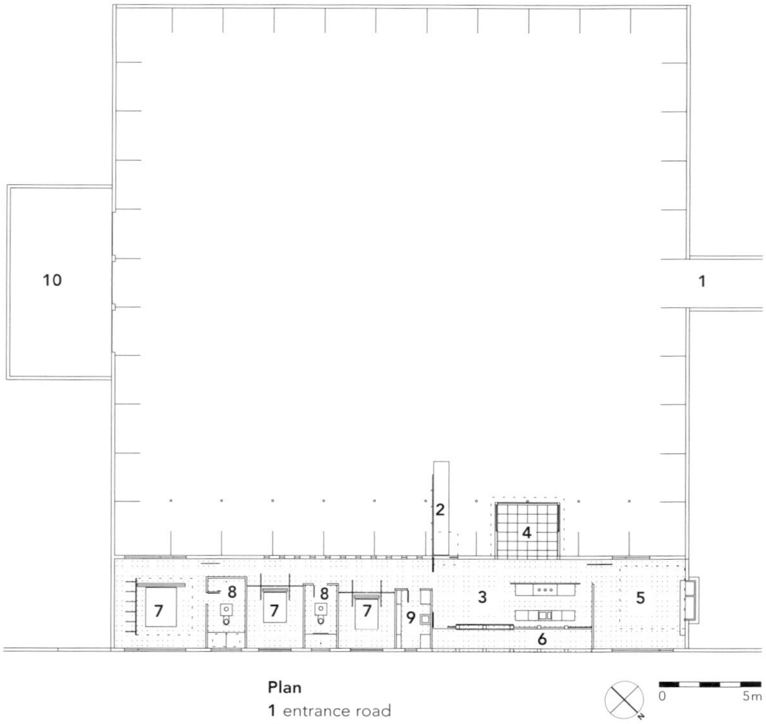

Plan
1 entrance road
2 entrance
3 kitchen/dining area
4 wintergarden
5 living room
6 loggia
7 bedroom
8 bathroom
9 laundry room
10 garage

On the courtyard side, near the entrance door, a galvanized steel sheet, one centimeter thick, orients the gaze toward the ocean while also protecting the courtyard from the coastal winds.

Like a cloister buried in nature, the house departs from notions of residence and domesticity.

The living room, furnished with the famous Sinbad sofa by Vico Magistretti, opens wide to the sea. The kitchen, with a loggia in front of it, adjoins the living room.

In one of the bedrooms, the steel bed by the architects, who designed most of the furniture.

A series of low, narrow windows (one meter tall by 30 centimeters wide) distill the light in the hall off the bedrooms. By showcasing the play of shadows on the ground, the windows chart the hours of the day.

Buried House in Moledo, Portugal

Eduardo Souto de Moura

In the tradition of Portuguese architects Fernando Távora and Alvaro Siza, the architecture of Eduardo Souto de Moura introduces modernity into the memory of the place, be it the urban fabric or a natural setting.
The house in Moledo showcases a distant view of the Atlantic Ocean while also forging a complex relationship with its immediate setting: a hill with terraces and old retaining walls of stone.
Like other houses built by Siza and Souto de Moura, the design required several years of thought and a close dialogue with the client. During these meetings, the program and the siting were gradually adjusted.
To make a connection with the granite rock of the slope, the architect set the house among the terraced layers, thus making it disappear on the hillside, after slightly adjusting its line to make room for a platform. The building sits on this platform, up against the rocks. Although it is bolstered by the presence of the strong contemporary architecture, the natural setting seems untouched, merely punctuated by the deliberate emergence of a long, flat concrete roof, which echoes the sea and the horizon.
From the bottom of the hill, a path leads to the entrance on the main façade, which is itself wedged in a retaining wall and oriented toward the sea.
The windows underline this feeling of fusion with the stone plane, and their proportions clarify the framing. Whether one looks toward the sea or away from it, toward the rocky slope that offers a protective screen for the bedrooms, the two façades are entirely glazed so that nature and the rocks visually invade the whole house. The front façade widens the gaze to the horizon; the rear façade draws it to the nearby environment, to the land and cold, mineral roughness of the hill.
Delineated by the concrete slab and the long horizontal line of the roof, which traces a new terrace, all the living spaces are on the same level. The large, light-filled living room takes up one-third of the surface area. Warmed by several touches of wood, the room is enlivened by a large granite wall that acts as an extension of the exterior walls. In this reworked fragment of the landscape, a minimalist approach showcases the countryside, and the contrasting materials reinforce this course of action.

Location: Moledo, Portugal — Program: family house incorporating, on one story, a large living/dining area, three bedrooms, two bathrooms, and a kitchen — Owner: António Reis — Architect: Eduardo Souto de Moura; Manuela Lara, Pedro Reis, Nuno Rodrigues Pereira, collaborators — Technical consultant for structure: José Adriano Cardoso — Surface area: 170 m² — Cost of work: 350,000 euros — Schedule: design, 1991; construction, 1998 — Building system and materials: concrete slab, steel, glass, and wood.

The horizontal roof, in tension with the sea and the horizon. "The roof should be exposed to view and announce itself as a new object, visible as if it had fallen from the sky."

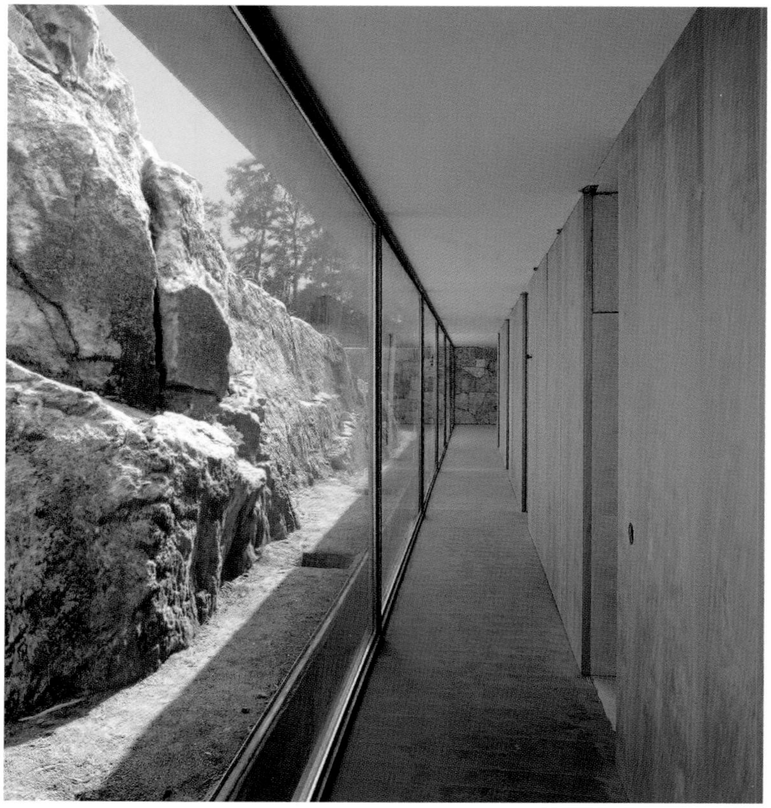

Contrast between the concrete floors, the glazing, and the wood when the light hits the rock to illuminate the rooms in the rear.

Note the optical illusion when the rocks are reflected in the windows on the rear façade. A passageway separates the house from the slope.

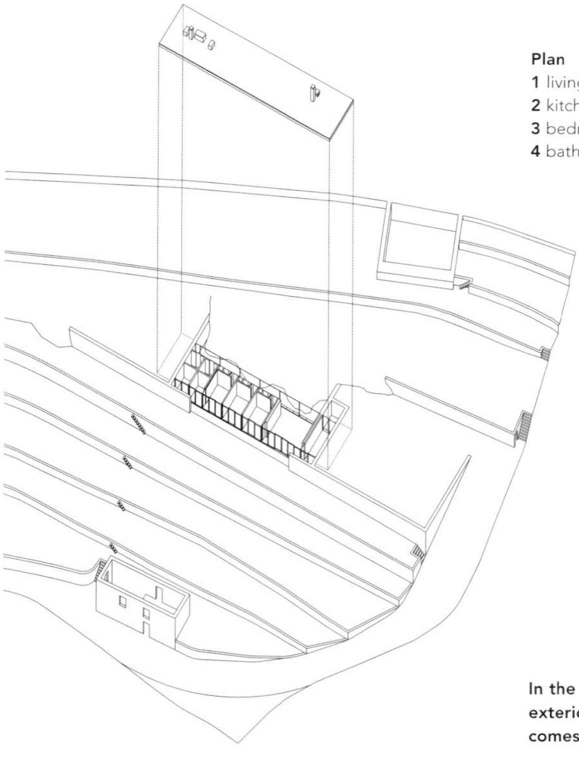

Plan
1 living/dining area
2 kitchen
3 bedroom
4 bathroom

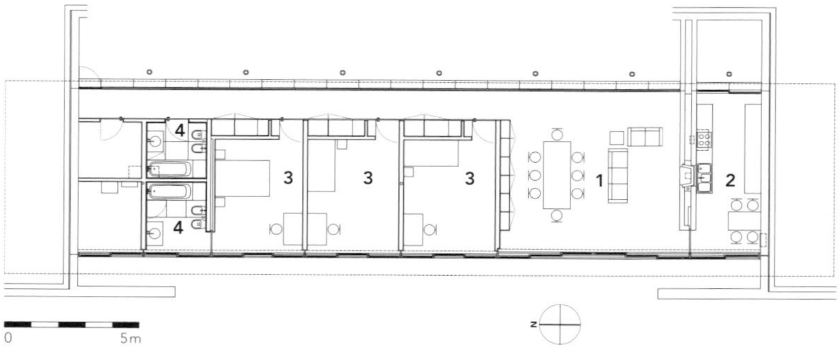

In the extension of the exterior walls, the stone comes into the living room.

Hardly visible in the stone wall, the long glazed façade takes in a wide view of the sea.

The entrance, entirely glazed. Owing to its transparency, the house draws the landscape inside.

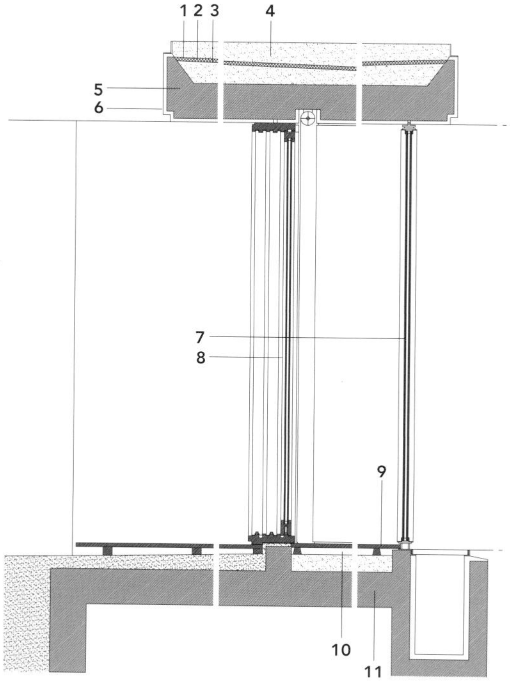

Detail of the glazed façades
1 drainage membrane
2 thermal insulation
3 waterproofing
4 concrete coating
5 concrete slab
6 plaster
7 stainless-steel frame
8 wood frame
9 wood floor
10 underfloor heating
11 concrete slab

Crater House in Antiparos, Greece

Deca Architecture

Seaside houses and movies often go well together. Inspired by a scene from Michelangelo Antonioni's *Zabriskie Point*, the architects thought of making this house – set at the summit of a hill in Antiparos, the smallest island of the Cyclades chain – crouch in a "livable crater," inexorably linked to the countryside that encircles it. Beyond the inventiveness of the idea, the key components of the design were the topography, the exposure criteria, and the reliance on local building techniques.
"The beauty of this landscape was intriguing," said the architects. "Our first goal was to explore the spirit of the place in order to entertain a dialectical relationship between our intervention and the existing environment. The aim was not to design a building that would adapt to the site but rather to create an event driven by the power of the setting. The location created a double constraint, however: not only did we have to protect the outdoor spaces from powerful breezes from the Aegean Sea, but we also had to hide the house at the top of the hill in order to preserve the unencumbered views, to which the villagers are attached. Thus the idea of a crater came naturally, having materialized through the exterior designs that were hidden away in the landscape to mark a buried space protected from the wind. In the hollow of the crater, a two-story stone volume offers protection against the northeast breezes that prevail in summer. Only the second story, in traditional quarry-stone masonry, is visible from the village."
The architects analyzed a model of the topography and the views in order to define the layout of the crater and the path of a "lava flow" that structures the architectural promenade. The section drawings made it possible to specify how the four main components of the residence – the stone, the "lava flow," the white prism, and the water – would intermingle. Each component found meaning in the composition with its own function. The stone marks the boundaries of the crater. On the north, a double-height quarry-stone volume, intended for the bedrooms and living spaces, offers protection from the wind. On the east, the walls surround the crater, forming the access ramp. A second volume with a steel structure rises on the south, supporting a bamboo roof. And the west opens to the sea.
The idea of a lava flow inspired a layout of a path running under the swimming pool and leading to the guest house. It is bordered by stone walls that spread apart to make room for a small, narrow garden.
The guest house comprises two sheltered spaces connected by a courtyard: one visible bedroom and one buried bedroom. The long white prism in the center of the crater houses the dining room and areas for socializing.
Finally, the water corresponds to the 25-meter swimming pool that runs around one side of the crater, directly in line with a small island north of Antiparos. At its western corner, an infinity effect gives swimmers the feeling of visual continuity between the water in the pool and the surface of the sea.

A scene from *Zabriskie Point*, a film by Michelangelo Antonioni, inspired the architects with idea of a lifestyle and landscape at the seaside.

Location: Antiparos Island, Cyclades, Greece — Program: house with a swimming pool and terrace, on three levels comprising a living room, kitchen, dining room, four bedrooms, six bathrooms, a semi-open room under a pergola, a barbecue room, utility rooms and closets, laundry area, and office; guest house comprising two bedrooms, a bathroom, and patio — Owner: Antiparos Design Properties, Oliaros SA — Architect: Deca Architecture — Surface area: building, 570 m²; outdoor covered areas, 125 m²; outdoor paved areas, 735 m² — Cost of work: not disclosed — Schedule: design, December 2001; completion, July 2004 — Building system and materials: structure in reinforced concrete, masonry walls, traditional plaster surface treatments for the white parts; reinforced-concrete structure, masonry shell and self-supporting stone walls for the portions in stone — General contractor: Nikos Kagelis.

At mid-route lies the white prism, where, on the far side, the large sliding doors blur the boundaries between indoors and outdoors. The kitchen window, at left, frames selected views of the swimming pool and the small neighboring islands.

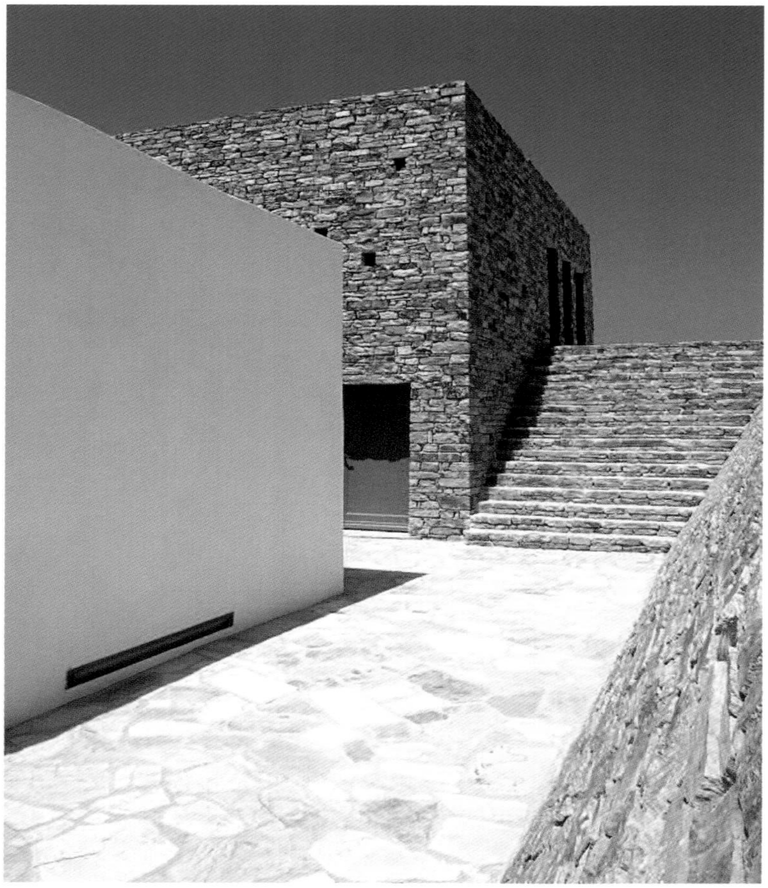

The "lava flow," bordered by a band of plants on the left, during the day, then at night.

Night view from the village; to preserve the beauty of the landscape, the house is buried, hardly visible.

In this work, the floor and the frame are equally important.

The contrast of the materials and the components, as well as the formal purity, borders on the abstract.

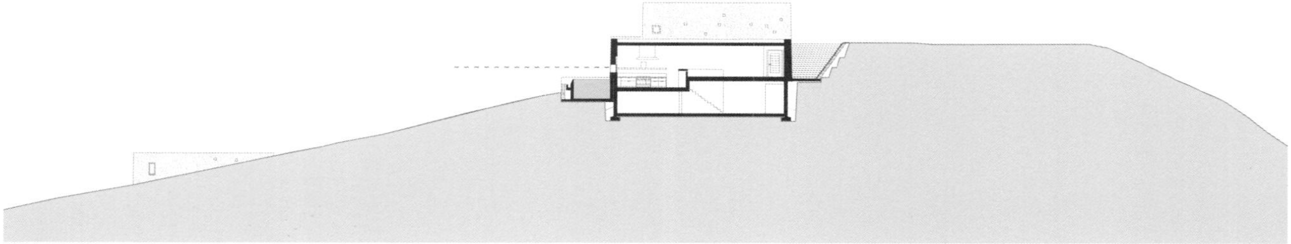

Section through the crater and the white prism.

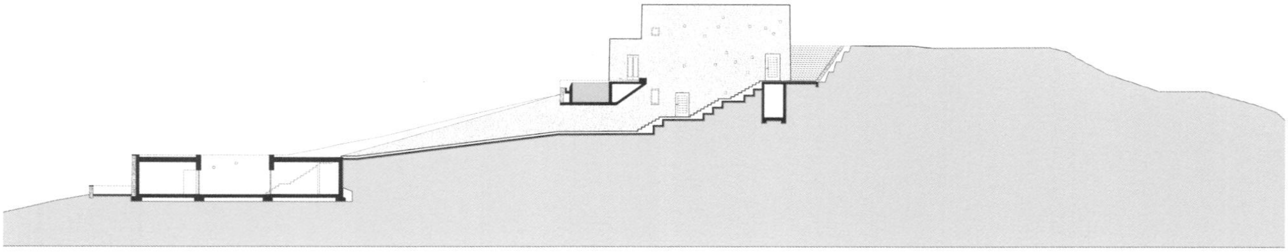

Section through the crater and the stone building.

0 5 10 m

1 living room
2 bedroom
3 bathroom
4 kitchen
5 dining room
6 semi-open room under a pergola
7 barbecue area
8 terrace
9 swimming pool
10 equipment room/ utility room
11 laundry room
12 closets
13 office

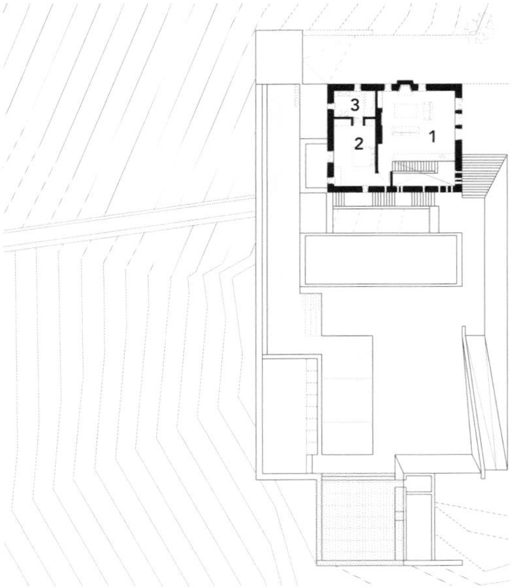

Upper-floor plan.

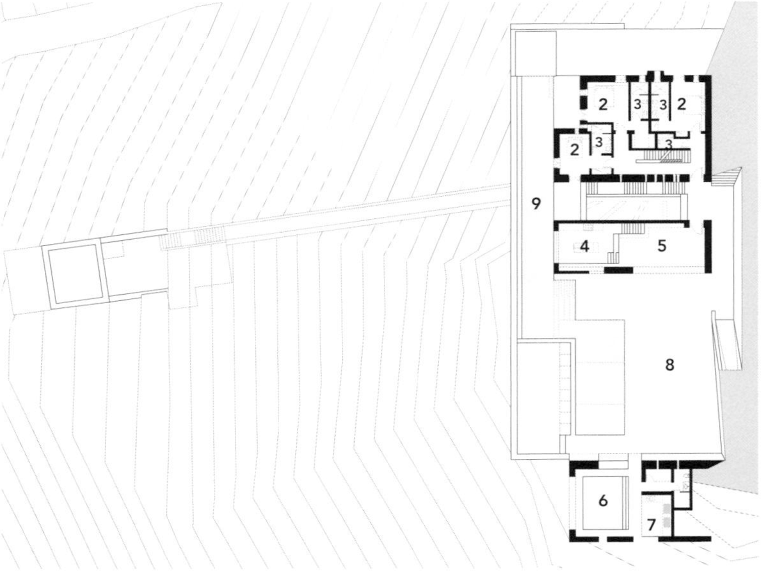

Ground-floor plan.

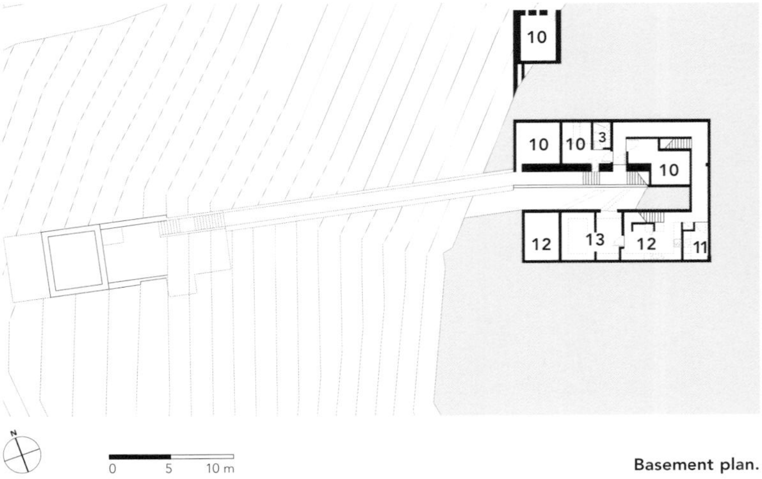

Basement plan.

Above:
Dining room and, in the background, the kitchen.

Below:
In the circulation areas, the periodic openings regulate the light and arrange unexpected framing.

Outdoors, various places to eat or relax, in the sun or under the rattan canes of a pergola.

House with an Organic Roof in Loredo, Spain

Nolaster arquitectos

With its organic roof that blends into the site without disrupting the visual continuity of the horizon line, this house resembles an elegantly designed object. Set on pilotis in the center of a sheltered garden dug out of a 30-meter-high cliff that is battered by the waves, it tames the natural topography and climate by defining its own territory. Unlike most of the neighboring houses, it can thus open to the sea while also finding protection from the violent wind that blows on the Cantabrian coast, near Santander.

One of the few sites available for building, this 90-by-50-meter parcel was subject to very strict regulations that reduced the occupied area to 8 percent of the site and limited its height. These restrictions dictated the form of the building, on a square plan of 22 meters on each side. The upper-floor volume, less than 3.5 meters tall, houses the main functions. It covers a ground floor that opens onto the garden and features the garage, laundry area, utility room, and spaces protected from the wind.

The program is distinctive: originally designed as a second home, the house can accommodate an extended family, up to twenty-six people for vacations or weekends. In the end, it became the main residence of the owners. A house for a couple, a summer house, a winter house, a house for hosting without getting in the way of friends and all the generations of a family, a house for short or long stays... To meet the expectations of their clients, the architects gave themselves three constraints: spatial simplicity, flexibility, and energy conservation. Starting from the idea of the typology of the unit, they divided the program into a series of strips running parallel to the ocean.

The strip closest to the ocean houses the library/living/dining area; the furthest, the guest rooms. The post-and-beam frame in stainless steel favors the modular nature of the spaces. The frame is characterized by an absence of color, and the rooms, separated by patios, can be adapted to various uses that may evolve over time, as is suggested by their sometimes unusual names: the Santander room, the bathroom/closet, the double bathroom, the room with many views, the vertical patio, the north hall, the entry patio, the introverted room, the indiscreet bathroom, the little space, the flexible space, the open bathroom, the tube room, the empty patio, the south hall, the fern patio, the multipurpose room... There are multiple routes linking all the rooms together, and linking the garden level, the upper floor, and the roof terrace. The steel façades on the three sides that do not look to the sea, furnished with movable perforated shutters, also add to the modular nature of the space. When the shutters are closed on one of the patios, the inhabitants have a new room, open to the sky and protected from the wind. The first work by the young Spanish firm Nolaster arquitectos, the house is one of ten projects selected by the jury of the ninth Exposition of Young Spanish Architects, organized by the Antonio Camuñas Foundation.

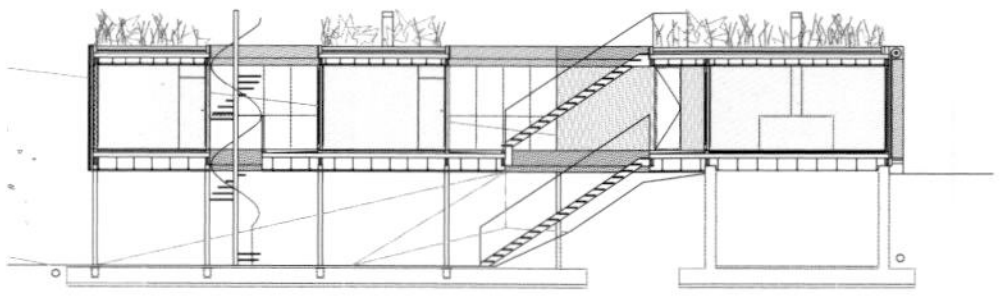

Location: Loredo, Spain — Program: large weekend house with a garage comprising a library/living/dining area, kitchen, multipurpose rooms, bedrooms, and bathrooms to accommodate up to twenty-six people — Owner: Carmen Salgado, José Miguel Oriol — Architect: Nolaster arquitectos; Arturo Romero, Beatriz G. Casares, Marcos González, Pablo Oriol, Fernando Rodríguez — Surface area: 496 m^2 — Cost: 1,070 euros per m^2 — Schedule: January 2004 – July 2005 — Materials: steel, zinc, glass, plasterboard, wood — Contractor: Construcciones Volga and Ramiro Bra.

The architects favor the relationship with the landscape. The organic roof is the most visible plane. It delineates a platform inscribed in the site. There is no chimney, and no other component protrudes above the horizon line.

The patios and the zenithal openings bring light into the center of the house.

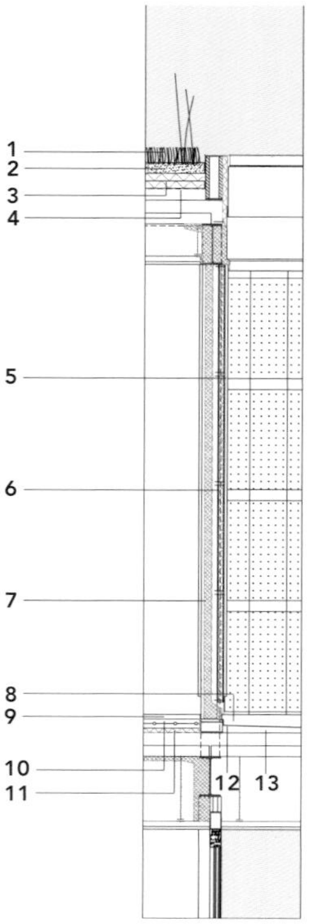

Detail of the façade arrangement. Articulation with the pilotis, the roof, and the metallic shutters.
1 organic roof, 15 cm thick
2 textile device, root control
3 double insulation
4 waterproofing
5 cement coating
6 agglomerated panels, 35 mm thick
7 insulation
8 drainage slab
9 wood flooring, 25 mm thick
10 underfloor heating
11 expanded polystyrene
12 asphalt
13 concrete slab

A bedroom, seen from the patio; in the background, the living room opening to the sea.

The shutters on the patios close to create new spaces that are protected from the wind in the extension of the rooms.

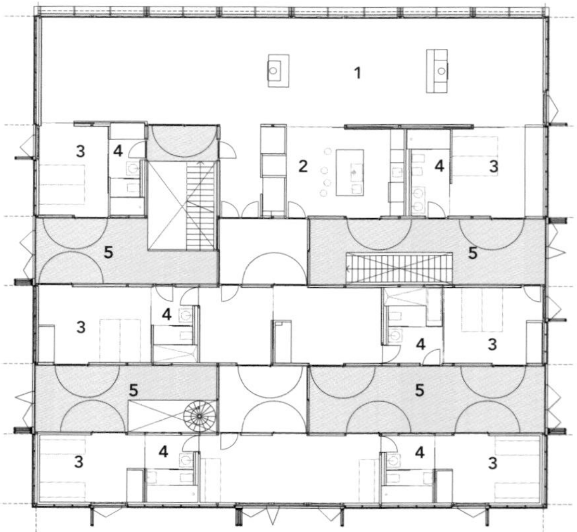

Upper-floor plan
1 library/living/dining area
2 kitchen
3 bedroom
4 bathroom
5 circulation/patio

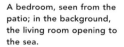

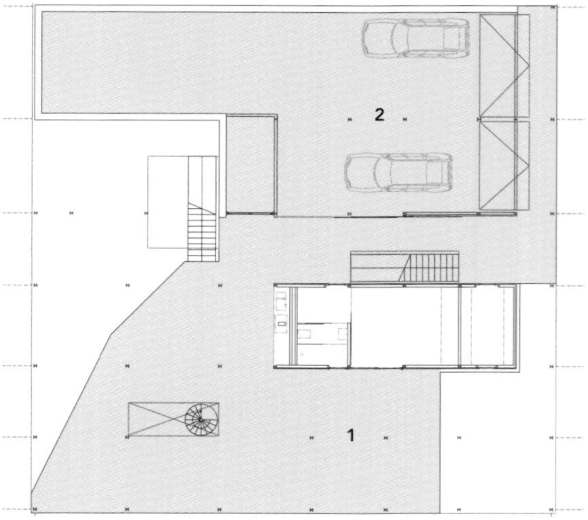

Ground-floor plan
1 covered terrace
2 garage

On the ground floor, one can sit outside, facing the garden and sheltered from the wind, under the upper-floor volume.

On the northwest, the opening to the sea provides the living room with a panoramic view of the landscape.

The structural frame gives rhythm to the space and promotes flexibility of use.

Siting, Structures, and Building Materials along the Shore

Key points and recommendations
When siting a seaside house, it is crucial to consider the orientation with regard to the sun and the prevailing winds, given the impact of these variables on the thermal and energy performance of the structure. This is especially true for out-of-the-way sites, where the houses cannot take advantage of the protection provided by shared walls.
The freedom of the plan and a certain spatial versatility promotes flexibility of uses in these houses, which are generally vacation homes. Thus, with a thick façade and sliding partitions, the house can be transformed in no time at all. Or the program can be distributed over several levels on a slope – which promotes uses that evolve with the seasons and the number of people present. Or the bedrooms can be set off in a specific volume. Or certain functions, especially the rooms with running water, can be set in a secondary strip in order to free up space for the living areas.
Everywhere, the structural options that further these principles should be adapted to the environment and to the abilities of the local contractors. At uneven or occasionally very remote sites, let us not forget the accessibility of the construction site if using a concrete mixer, having prefabricated components delivered, or inspecting the work along the way. The building materials (glass, copper, polymers, wood, concrete, steel, and stone), the plaster, and the paint should be used with good judgment, and the details carefully designed and executed. They all should be resistant to the sea air: special paint, steel treated against corrosion, and so on. It is also appropriate to find out about the health aspects of the products used in the finishes (intrinsic quality and durability), with a preference for natural materials that do not pose a health risk.
Starting at the design phase, one should try to limit heat loss and, to do so, analyze the energy balance of the materials and the cost of energy, adjusting for the regional specificities in order to choose an adequate method of heating. The different technical and architectural options, as well as the specific thermal features of various materials, make it possible more or less to retain heat in winter and to regulate it in summer. In this regard, various protective strategies exist (exterior sun protection, organic screens, awnings, pergolas, shutters, persian blinds, reduction in the size of the openings, and so on). We recommend avoiding air conditioning in favor of natural ventilation devices that are more suitable for today's great environmental challenges. On the residential scale, installing solar or photovoltaic collectors or a geothermal heating system requires a substantial investment and a projected cost estimate that is precise. By contrast, the common-sense rules and simple massing of vernacular structures are an inexhaustible source of inspiration to get into the mentality of a place and to introduce ad hoc contemporary architecture.
Finally, as these houses are not always occupied year-round, the technical options should maintain security and minimize upkeep when the house is empty. Thus it is necessary to find clever ways to keep the sand from entering (by raising the floor slightly, for example) and installing mosquito screens or other devices to protect the house from insects, birds, and rodents.

Concrete
This technical information was prepared in collaboration with Roland Dallemagne, a consultant, former representative of CIMbéton, and former managing editor of the journal *Construction moderne*.

Owing to its structural and plastic performance, and also to the quality of the material, concrete is often used in seaside houses. Poured in place, it affords great freedom in terms of shapes and openings, and all the masons in the world know how to work with it using the materials on the shore. With concrete, it is possible to create thick walls, which are valuable for thermal comfort, as well as large, thin walls or curved partitions, facilitating the siting on the landscape. To avoid corrosion of the reinforcements, the contractors reduce the water density (the recommended water/cement ratio for ready-mix concrete is 0.55) and increase the concrete cover thickness of the standard concrete. They also optimize the structural durability by following the recommendations of Eurocode 2 and those of the standard NF EN 206-1. As the chemical and physical properties of the material have changed dramatically over the past years with the contribution of additives and plasticizers, the new types of concrete have become very successful. By improving the cement grain hydration, porosity is reduced, and the material becomes much denser and more resistant over the long term. The water/cement ratio has changed with the growing use of additives that help improve the plasticity without the need for much water. Walls can naturally be left as struck, but the surface treatments allow for many different looks: rough, smooth, with a raised design, decorated with motifs, and so on. One final advantage: concrete walls do not require any special upkeep.

• *Thermal and ecological performance*
In order to reduce the impact on greenhouse gases each year within the context of the Kyoto Protocol, by 2050 France, for example, aims to reduce by a factor of four the 9 tons of annual CO_2 emissions per inhabitant. The new thermal regulations, called RT 2005 for new buildings, went into effect on September 1, 2006, lowering the maximum energy consumption allowed. In this context, the architect can, starting in the design phase, single out one of the main characteristics of concrete, namely, its thermal inertia, described as "heavy." Through its strong heat capacity, this material can store heat or cold, then release them as needed. Thanks to this property, which is associated with appropriate heat ventilation, it is possible to limit the discomforts of summer and reduce heat consumption in winter.

Wood
This information was prepared in collaboration with Marion Cloarec, head of development at the CNDB (National Committee for the Development of Wood in France).

An ecological material and a readily available renewable resource, wood is currently used throughout the world. Wood houses are common on the seaside, especially in Nordic countries. The post-beam-floor frames, like the light timber framing technique, allow for great freedom in the plan, which lends itself well to vacation homes.
Wood is not sensitive to salt. Along the shore, people generally choose a wood that can be left in a natural state or painted. Red resinous heartwood, such as Scots, or maritime pine, or Douglas fir, but also oak, chestnut, and locust, meet these requirements. Traditionally, in Nordic countries, rich paints made of fish oil and mineral pigments are applied. For maximum protection, the very exposed wood of the façades is soaked in tar. These surface applications, which are regularly reapplied, have the advantage of letting the wood breathe. Its durability depends on it.
Simple in appearance, the timber-frame building nevertheless requires great exactness and precision in the execution of details. Above all, water traps must be eliminated: water should always be able to flow in order to avoid weakening a structure, especially when the wood is left exposed. For attaching weatherboarding, the use of stainless-steel ring shank nails is obligatory in order to avoid streaks of rust. These recommendations are universal; however, in different regions and different climates, local craftsmen often give good advice. Another advantage of wood: it is possible to prefabricate a certain number of components, which could possibly be delivered by boat if the coastal area is difficult to access.

• *Thermal and ecological performance*
This is the era of moderation in energy use, and wood, which is naturally very insulating, contributes to it. The lambda, λ, of a material is calculated in watt per meter per Celsius degree (W/m.°C), which determines its thermal conductivity. Resiniferous trees, which are used mainly for the frame and the envelope of wood structures, have low thermal conductivity, between 0.13 and 0.15. For the sake of comparison, the lambda of mineral wool is 0.04, that of steel is 52, and that of aluminum soars to 230. The standards take into account the conductivity of the whole wall in determining the energy properties. The coefficient U defines the conductivity of the partition (Up), wall, or floor. The RT 2005 thermal regulation recommends a Up of 0.36 and authorizes a maximum of 0.45. A timber-frame wall falls between 0.32 and 0.34, depending on the choice of insulation; this constitutes very good performance.

• *Building houses in pine along the Aquitaine coast*
This information was prepared in collaboration with Hadrien Bartherotte, director of Cabanes Bartherotte & Frères.

The southwestern part of France is a large forested region and yet, there is no choice but to admit that the local pine wood is hardly valued for construction. For the frame, whitewood is preferred, and for the floors, exotic wood from Brazil, Africa, and Asia is often used; this affects the local economy and seems totally preposterous in terms of transportation costs and ecology. Faithful to the adage of their father, for whom "wood should not be treated but rather well treated," the children of Benoît Bartherotte, at the helm of the company Cabanes Bartherotte & Frères, build houses near Arcachon that are made of Landes pine. The houses obey some simple rules:
– start with the building principle that the form of each house is unique. It is adapted to the site and respects a wooded environment where existing trees are preserved;
– all structures are made of pine from the Landes region, preferably resinous pine, as old as possible. Each part of the tree is carefully selected according to its use in the future house: the longest pieces are reserved for the floorboards and weatherboarding, the most knotty for the framework, the reddest (in heartwood, without sapwood) for the parts most exposed to humidity (bathrooms, kitchens, and decks);
– the post-and-beam building system, consisting of loadbearing posts, wood floors, and a rough-sawn-pine frame in sections cut to measure, does not require a concrete slab or loadbearing wall. The structure sits on blocks, leaving room for a crawl space under the house. Because there is no contact with the ground, it is possible to avoid an upwelling of moisture. In areas with termites, the treatment and protection of the floors is obligatory;
– the construction requires approximately 1,500 tenons and mortises for an average-size unit. The hardware, in bronze or brass, ages at the same pace as the wood, without any risk of corrosion. The furniture, kitchen, bathrooms, wood floors, and windows, also of pine, are made to measure in the studio, which makes it possible to create nonstandard doors and windows. The electrical and plumbing systems are concealed with special care;
– thermal and sound insulation is natural: no glass wool or petroleum derivatives. Priority is given to hemp, cork, and wood fiber;
– for heating, depending on the situation, installation of an electric boiler with heat inertia, gas central heating, or wood-pellet boiler – an affordable and renewable fuel – to promote biomass.

Protecting the Coast

Protecting coastal landscapes without hindering the economic development of the countries is a planetary challenge; throughout the world, there are many preservation authorities capable of orchestrating ambitious projects and continually developing legislation.

Founded in 1948, the World Conservation Union (known by its French acronym, IUCN), headquartered in Switzerland, brings together close to a thousand governmental and nongovernmental members from eighty countries to define the policies and programs for the protection and preservation of nature as a whole. Ten thousand scientists work in partnership there. The IUCN manages ecosystems so as to protect biodiversity and promote sustainable development. It has helped more than seventy-five countries develop national conservation strategies for natural sites.

A private organization founded in 1895 to acquire and protect threatened coastal land, sites, and buildings, the National Trust was the first institution to work on a national scale, and it serves as the model for many others. The trust conducts a policy of acquisition and protection of coastal and rural areas as well as remarkable monuments. Working in England, Wales, and Northern Ireland, it now oversees 248,000 hectares and approximately 1,300 kilometers of coastal land, which is almost 10 percent of the shores of Great Britain. On the coasts, the National Trust essentially tries to conduct a dynamic policy against erosion and the rising sea level. The Neptune Coastline Campaign, launched in 1965, aims to save the most beautiful shores from uncontrolled development and tries to facilitate access to them.

A public institution created in 1975, the Conservatoire du littoral et des rivages lacustre (known in English as the Coastal Protection Agency) was inspired by the British National Trust to conduct land-use policies aimed at definitively protecting natural areas and shores. The agency covers coastal areas in France, French overseas departments, the island of Mayotte, and the banks of estuaries, deltas, and lakes of 1,000 hectares or more.

The primary landowner of the French coasts, it acquires and restores natural spaces where building is not allowed; the organization also works to make these areas accessible to the public. As of January 1, 2007, 103,000 hectares, 880 kilometers of shoreline, and four hundred natural areas were under its control. A member of the World Conservation Union (IUCN), and of the Eurosite Association, it works with other conservation agencies in France, Europe, and throughout the world. The French Research Institute for Exploration of the Sea (known by its French acronym, IFREMER), created in 1982, has a site dedicated to monitoring the coastal environment.

For the past dozen years, the Coastal Protection Agency has conducted a policy of active cooperation with the countries of the Maghreb and has researched the creation of conservation agencies similar to those in Mediterranean countries.

These activities came to fruition, notably in Tunisia with the creation, in 1995, of the Tunisian National Agency for Coastal Protection and Planning (known by its French acronym, APAL). In this country, an international seminar was held in Mahdia in June 1999 on the subject of urban development in coastal areas.

Given the magnitude of what is currently at stake, conservation initiatives, regulations, and organizations continue to expand throughout the world. It is impossible to make an exhaustive inventory of them in a few lines; it will have to suffice to mention few key elements.

In Australia, there is no national conservation agency, but rather many specific conservation authorities for certain sites, such as the Sydney Bay Shore Authority, which oversees the Sydney Bay area.

The same is true in the United States, where specific authorities exist in the various states, such as the California Coastal Conservancy, which plays a key role in purchasing and protecting some coastal lands on the California coast.

Finally, in Japan, where getting a site on the sea is always an important concern, often to the detriment of the ecosystems, a framework law on the environment, adopted in the 1990s, has been working to make the population and the industrial and political players more aware of coastal protection.

Some useful web sites
www.conservatoire-du-littoral.fr
www.iucn.org
www.ifremer.fr
www.nationaltrust.org.uk
www.tunisie.com/environnement
www.unesco.org (for the proceedings of the international seminar held in Mahdia, published in 2000 by Unesco)

Photo Credits

Archikubik: 29 center left and bottom, 156.
Archives du monde du travail, Roubaix/Fonds Simounet: 24 center right and lower right, 25 center.
Jaime Ardiles-Arce: 11 top and center right.
Erietta Attali: 22.
Benoît Bartherotte: 17.
Hadrien Bartherotte: 157.
Jordi Bernado: 29 top right.
Hélène Binet: 108-11.
Brett Boardman: 30, 105-07.
Luc Boegly/Artedia: 21 center.
Richard Bryant/Arcaid: 25 top right and bottom right, 50-53.
Earl Carter: 13 bottom.
Frederic Cooper: 26 top and center right.
Jean-Pierre Crousse: 132-35.
Serge Demailly: 35-39.
Michel Denancé: 10 top left and bottom left.
Bernard Dubor: 13 top and center right.
Cemal Emden: 23 top left and right, 54-59.
Bengt Ericksson: 11 center left and bottom.
åke Eson/Lindman photography: 84-85, 90 top, 92 top right, 116-19.
Violeta Ferrand: 26 center left and bottom.
Luis Ferreira Alves: 143-45.
Klaus Frahm/Artur/Artedia: 8 top, 9.
Hayley Franklin: 13 center left.
Mitsumasa Futjisuka: 12 center, bottom left and bottom right.
Alfio Garozzo: 27 top and center.
Chris Gascoigne/View pictures: 112, 113, 114 top and center, 115.
John Gollings: 124-25, 136-41.
Kyle Gudsell: 147-51.
Roland Halbe: 31 bottom left and bottom right.
José Hevia: 152-55.
Alexander Kornhuber: 120-23.
Lacoste + Stevenson Architects: 104.
Mairie de Roquebrune-Cap-Martin: 21 top left and top right.
Olivier Martin-Gambier – FLC/Adagp/Artedia: 21 bottom left and bottom right.
Cristiano Mascaro: 15 bottom left and bottom right.
Yoshiharu Matsumura: 64-69.
Mitsuo Matsuoka: 87-89.
Shannon McGrath: 40-43.
Jean-Marie del Moral: 16.
Cristobal Palma: front cover, 31 top and center, 32-33, 44-49, 78-83.
Pere Planells: 24 top left and bottom left.
Undine Pröhl: 14 top left and bottom left.
Philippe Robert: 15 top.
Rue des archives: 8 bottom.
Andy Ryan: 94-96, 97 bottom left and bottom right.
Jacqueline Salmon: 20.
James Silverman: 91, 92 top left, center, and bottom, 93, 127-31.
Ambrose Snug: 114 bottom.
Ib Soerensen: 74-77.
Ezra Stoller/Esto: 18.
Jorgen Struwing: 10 right.
Studio Fuksas: 23 center, bottom left and bottom right.
M. Torimura/Nacasa & Partners Inc.: 99-103.
Leo Torri: 70-73.
Brian Vanden Brink: 61-63.
Jean-Paul Viguier: 12 top.
Philippe Vion: 14 right.
Paul Warchol: 28, 97 top.
Stella Watmough: 27 bottom.
Alan Weintraub/Arcaid: 19.
Nigel Young: 25 bottom left.